Tariffs and growth

Some illustrations from the world economy, 1850–1940

Forrest Capie

This book considers some of the historical experience of protectionism in the world economy, and shows how it can be applied to the problems of the world economy today.

Protectionism in international trade has been a recurrent feature of the trade of nations for at least two hundred years. It is topical today, with the Gatt negotiations, growing protectionism in the OECD countries, and the need for policy solutions for the problems of Russia, Eastern Europe, and the Central Asian Republics.

Forrest Capie traces the fluctuating fortunes of free trade as against protectionism from the nineteenth century to the middle of the twentieth. He looks at the origins of the protectionist case and the circumstances in which it came to be adopted and in which it sometimes flourished. He shows that protectionism has commonly been coupled with nationalism and been associated with major calamities in the world economy.

Tariffs and growth will be of interest to economists, policy makers, economic historians, and students of trade and international economic relations.

Forrest Capie is Professor of Economic History at the City University Business School, London

Insights from Economic History
General editor: Nick Crafts

This series makes accessible major results from recent research in economic history, with an emphasis on issues of current importance. The books present an authoritative and objective view of the 'lessons of history' for the non-expert, while comprising essential reference material for the professional economic historian. The focus of the series is on issues in economic history that have contemporary relevance for policy-makers and for economists wishing for a digest of key research results.

Also in the series

Barry Eichengreen
Reconstructing Europe's trade and payments: the European Payments Union

Forrest H. Capie

Tariffs and growth

Some illustrations from the world economy 1850–1940

Manchester University Press
Manchester and New York
Distributed exclusively in the USA and Canada by St Martin's

Published by Manchester University Press
Oxford Road, Manchester M13 9PL, UK
and Room 400, 175 Fifth Avenue, New York, NY10010, USA

Distributed exclusively in the USA and Canada
by St. Martin's Press Inc., 175 Fifth Avenue, New York, NY 10010, USA

British Library Cataloguing-in-Publication Data
A catalogue record for this book is available from the British Library

Library of Congress Cataloging-in-Publication Data
Capie, Forrest.
Tariffs and growth : some illustrations from the world economy, 1850–1940 / Forrest Capie.
p. cm.—(Insights from economic history)
ISBN 0–7190–3937–1 (cloth).—ISBN 0–7190–3938–X (paper)
1. Tariff—History. 2. Protectionism—History. 3. Economic history—1750–1918. 4. Economic history—1918–1945. I. Title. II. Series.
HF1711.C36 1994
382′.7—dc20 93–35901

ISBN–0 7190 3937 1 *hardback*
0 7190 3938 X *paperback*

Photoset in Linotron Sabon by
Northern Phototypesetting Co Ltd., Bolton
Printed in Great Britain by
Biddles Ltd., Guildford and King's Lynn

Contents

Tables and figures

Tables

Figures

Preface

This short book considers some of the historical experience of protectionism the world economy, to show not only how useful, but how necessary, some historical knowledge of the issue is. From the length of the book alone it will be obvious that this is not a history of protection. Instead, an attempt has been made to try to use some past experience to highlight the principal dangers that are present in the world economy, and to remind us that we are not immune from the dangers. Some of the major episodes in the period 1850–1940 are drawn on to illustrate how protection has come to be adopted, what it has meant for the individual countries adopting it, as also for the international economy, and to bring out the similarities in some repeated experience.

I should like to thank David Henderson for his comments on a first draft. He was responsible for my reshaping some of the underlying argument, particularly in persuading me to adjust my views on the power of interest groups. I should also like to thank Max Corden, Brian Hindley, Geoffrey Wood and the editor of the series, Nick Crafts, all of whose comments on the first draft led to substantial improvements. None of them is, of course, in any way responsible for the remaining deficiencies. I should also like to thank Tad Rybczynski for his verbal comments, since his hand-written comments went astray in the internal mail!

F.C.
May 1993

Chapter 1

Introduction

The rebirth of protectionism

The late 1980s and early 1990s have seen the collapse of planned economies around the world. And now that more is known about them their economic performance turns out to have been even worse than their critics had believed. Not only that, but their faults seem to have been greater than those of the market economies – pollution, corruption and so on. There is therefore surely something of a paradox. For just as these countries have been overturning regulation and looking to embrace the market economy to derive the economic and political benefits of freedom, in the market economies some regulation of activity and management of the economy have been reappearing.

Nowhere is this more true than in the field of international trade. Not only has there emerged a 'new' international trade theory that argues that protectionism ('sophisticated intervention') can be a superior policy stance, but protectionist sentiment has been greatly on the rise, and protectionist measures have been increasing throughout the Western world economy. It was once accepted – indeed, it was the conventional wisdom – that the great growth of output and trade in the post-World War II economy went hand in hand with the liberalisation of that economy, and that the reason for liberalisation lay in learning from the mistakes of the inter-war years. The mistakes were widely regarded as being the protectionist commercial and associated policies, and the lack of trust that these bred in international affairs.

That lesson appears to have been forgotten or dismissed. There is no doubt that protectionism has been on the increase in the last twenty years. The IMF's 1975 *Report on Exchange Restrictions* was the first of its kind to find more increases than decreases in the number of restrictions. All the reports for the rest of the decade recorded more restrictions. That process has continued to be charted in the IMF's annual publications. Not only has the number of restrictions increased but their coverage has been extended, so that the proportion of world trade that falls under some form of control has become even larger. The extent is often difficult to estimate precisely, but there is general agreement that the trend has been distinctly upward, particularly in the OECD countries.

When in January 1992 the Russians announced they were erecting trade barriers against the former republics of the Soviet Union they provoked what can only be described as an affectation of dismay among some Western commentators. It is surely an affectation, since many of these commentators have supported the advocacy of planned or managed or strategic trade.

At one level the observation of individual increases in protection could be regarded with equanimity and seen as being of less importance than might at first sight be imagined. But at another level it is potentially damaging. It is less important in the sense that (1) the increases frequently have only a small impact, and (2) ways are invariably found of evading regulations of any kind, such that sometimes the regulation is defeated. Regulation does nevertheless involve a misallocation of resources, and this is as true of protectionism as it is of any other form. The economic impact of protection is difficult to determine but it is fair to say that protection does not appear to have raised the performance of economies employing it; nor, on the other hand, does it appear to have done great harm to the individual economy adopting it. However, protection has damaged many economies, particularly those heavily dependent on exports, and there are many examples, particularly among the less developed countries, of suffering as a result of manufacturing protection. One of the most obvious is India; and there are countries such as New Zealand suffering as a result of widespread agricultural protection. Further, the spread of protectionism which has invariably followed from apparently small moves in that direction has proved costly. At the present time this is true particularly of developing or primary producing countries. The implementation of some protectionist measures by one important trading country is soon followed by measures by others, irrational though that may be, and then usually accompanied by allegations of unfair trading practice.

The distrust that follows can degenerate into open accusation and eventually lead to a breakdown of the world economy. Something like this has been the experience of the modern world economy that dates from the middle of the nineteenth century. Currently the world economy seems to have embarked upon yet another surge of protectionism which if not halted is surely in danger of going the way of previous experience. If there are any doubts on this score a quick perusal of recent American pronouncements on the subject should be enough to worry even the most sanguine. The only bright spot on the horizon is the liberalisation that has been taking place in less developed countries, and in some regional arrangements. These were the countries where the highest rates of protection prevailed until the mid-1980s, where there was greatest scope for reduction, and where most actual reduction has take place.

The lessons

The above remarks suggest that there may be lessons that can be learnt from history. How far can this idea be taken? History can be thought of as society's memory, even if it is accepted that we learn only slowly and imperfectly from experience, and on occasions not at all. Simple perversity or failure to comprehend and/or agree upon what is happening, and has happened, may result in recurring damage being inflicted on oneself and on others.

In every area of the economy there are experiences that bear a resemblance to some previous experience. For example, fluctuations in economic activity – business cycles – have been occurring since at least the beginning of the industrial revolution in the eighteenth century. If this is so, and these fluctuations are costly, can lessons not be learned about what it is that causes them? Then action might be taken to prevent them. Remarkable though it may seem, there is still dispute over whether cycles exist, or at minimum what their precise dating is, never mind what causes them, and therefore there is still some problem over knowing what might be done to dampen them or – ideally – prevent them. Until there is some agreement about the genuine understanding of such phenomena there can be little prospect of minimising fluctuations, let alone preventing them.

Another example that is perhaps easier to deal with, the British economy, like others, was once beset by regular financial crises. Over time means were found and structures evolved that averted such events, and they were for a long time effectively eradicated – a clear case of learning from the past. A more recent episode was the stock market surge of the 1980s that culminated in the great boom and collapse of 1987. At least at first sight, this episode looked very much like that of the 1920s. So well known was the earlier episode, and so well researched and analysed, that a considerable amount of agreement prevailed on what to avoid doing in order to escape the feared great depression that the collapse might have heralded. It looks likely that the correct lessons were learned, particularly in the United States, and the appropriate action was taken. Nevertheless, it is important to remember that the two events, while similar, were not strictly comparable, and the world was a radically different place in the 1980s from what it was in the 1920s.

Learning lessons depends on first reaching agreement about the nature and causes of events, and hence on the appropriate prescriptive policies for situations that look like becoming repetitions of previous experience. The question that is addressed in this book is: can anything be learnt from experiences of protectionism in world trade? Can something be said about the way in which protectionism arises, and what it is that leads to it spreading in an apparently uncontrollable way? No two experiences will be the same, but there may be sufficiently strong similarities for parallels to be found, lessons drawn and policies devised.

Contents of this book

In this book, a short guide to the pattern of free trade and protection in the modern world economy is provided first. It is followed by an outline of some basic theory of international trade and discussion of how that helps in understanding the persistent calls for protection. The book then looks in turn at the two major periods of protection in the modern world economy – that is, in the world economy since 1850. The first was the period from about 1880 to the First World War. The second was the period between the two World Wars.

The first serious and prolonged outbreak of protection followed a reasonably long period in the middle of the century when free trade appeared to have triumphed. America, however, reverted to its more accustomed protectionism in the Civil War, 1861–65. And when Germany imposed tariffs in 1878 other countries followed, until eventually tariff wars broke out in the 1890s between at least some of the parties. In what follows we seek to uncover the origins of this growth in protection and to examine the effect it had on the countries implementing it. The origins, it is not surprising to find, owe a great deal to pressure groups. The extent of protection, however, turns out to have been less than is often suggested, and the impact on economic growth is found to have been trivial. However, protectionism cannot easily be separated from the nationalism that flourished, and together they led the world into war.

The second part of the experience is in the period between the two World Wars, and is usually portrayed as being quite different. Whereas the period from 1870 to 1914 is usually thought of as a long period of peace and economic progress, the years from 1919 to 1939 are seen as years of great turmoil, usually thought of as the years of the Great Depression and of poor performance generally. This is essentially true, but as far as commercial policy goes there are some parallels. The First World War did nothing to roll back the tide of nationalism that had developed before 1914 and was its fundamental cause. In fact in many ways the war exacerbated the nationalism. New nation states were born, as a consequence of the war. National awareness was therefore raised, and where formerly there had been domestic trade there was now international trade and there developed a desire for a degree of self-sufficiency. After outlining the background to the deterioration in international trading relations we turn to the interesting case of Britain, the original and principal exponent of the free-trade doctrine.

We consider the origins of the protectionist pressures, using Britain as a particular example, and ask why on this occasion – 1932 – the pressure was not resisted. The British economy performed exceptionally well in the 1930s, and we examine the part that the tariff played in this success. It turns out not to have been of importance for growth. But again, on the wider front, it is inescapable that international breakdown again occurred in the 1930s, and protectionism was in part responsible. The British example was not a good one, and it undoubtedly contributed to the darkening international climate.

The book does not pretend to be comprehensive. That would result in a huge volume. It does not touch on many countries, focusing on the principal European countries and the United States. Nor does it cover the period since the Second World War, on the grounds that the period up to the 1970s was one of increasing liberalisation of trade, and the period after that is the one we are trying to set in some historical perspective.

The central questions of interest are: how did protectionism arise in the past, and what was its impact?

Chapter 2

The pattern of protection in the world economy

This chapter outlines the pattern of alternating free-trade and protectionist regimes in the modern world economy, that is, from around the middle of the nineteenth century. There had, of course, been trade across frontiers for thousands of years, but there was nothing that could be considered as an integrated world economy until the nineteenth century. By then industrialisation was spreading and there were substantial flows of capital, and large movements of labour and goods.

From some time around the middle of the nineteenth century there has been a relatively well integrated world economy. At that time there were several industrialising countries, and many other primary producing countries that were becoming increasingly closely connected by virtue of growing trade, capital movements and flows of migrant labour. All these variables were to increase enormously in the last twenty or thirty years or so before the First World War. Trade was then severely disrupted and in some cases was terminated by the war. After 1918 trade was seriously affected by all the problems of post-war adjustment. That was followed by worldwide depression in the years 1929–33, and at the end of the 1930s again by war. It was not until after the Second World War that a period of further rapid growth in output took place and trade grew even faster, at unprecedented rates, for around two decades.

From the emergence of the modern world economy around the middle of the nineteenth century until the present day the world economy has gone through alternating periods of comparatively free trade and protection. Britain was the leading industrial nation at the hub of this emerging world economy in 1850 and had rejected protectionist policies in the 1840s. She had instead adopted free trade and then endeavoured to export the doctrine of free trade to the rest of the world. In the years from the 1840s to the 1860s many other countries moved in the same direction, so that the period from 1850 to the 1870s can be described as one of comparatively free trade. It was in 1860 that the Cobden–Chevalier treaty was signed between Britain and France, which signalled a breakthrough between two great trading rivals. The British example was quite widely accepted as demonstrating that free trade brought prosperity and others were keen to pursue the same course. In addition, Cobden's message that it also brought peace had a certain appeal.

But for a variety of reasons, some of which are considered below, there were many moves towards protection in the 1870s and 1880s. When Germany introduced protectionist legislation in 1879 it was a sign of a major shift away from free trade. The French followed in 1881, and then further with the Meline tariff and other measures in 1892. Italy was thoroughly protectionist in outlook by the 1890s and Russia, following some liberalisation in the 1860s, reverted to a highly protectionist stance by the 1890s. America had always inclined to protection but did move towards free trade in the decade before the Civil War. The Morrill tariff of 1861 revived protection in the United States and thereafter all the movement was in the direction of protection. Even the British dominions were protectionist by the end of the century. Growing protectionism and nationalism went together, so that the period from the late 1870s up to the First World War (some would argue culminating in the Great War) is usually characterised as protectionist.

The war did not resolve the problems of the world economy – indeed, in some important respects it aggravated them. New nations were born, old differences remained, and international distrust intensified in the 1920s and 1930s. Rising protectionism accompanied the suspicion and distrust, and resulted in the worsening of the intense nationalism that had lain behind the First World War. The Americans again set the pace, with the Fordney–McCumber tariff of 1922, and other countries quickly followed suit. The United States imposed further 'skyscraper' tariffs with the Smoot–Hawley legislation of 1930. When, in 1931 and 1932, the British abandoned the free-trade policies that they had held to for nearly a century and curtain had finally come down.

In Europe fascism emerged, with its emphasis on self-sufficiency and its bilateral trading philosophy. As some see it, the Second World War was not so much a second war as a continuation of the first, after an interlude full of tension.

The unhappy experience of the inter-war years with the associated depression made the allied countries determined to lay the foundations of a better, more secure and more prosperous world when the Second World War was over. The basis was to be a liberal world trading order. New institutions were designed and established to promote such an order. The International Monetary Fund was established to promote stable exchange rates. The General Agreement on Tariffs and Trade (GATT) was to promote tariff reduction and lead to an expansion of trade. This ambition of liberalisation and stability was largely successful, and the period from the late 1940s until about 1970 may be said to have been one of increasingly free trade, at least among the OECD countries, though still not in some important respects.

This picture of freedom should not be overdone, however. It is true that there was a widespread desire to promote trade and the economic growth that it was believed would follow. It is also true that institutional changes were instrumental in liberalising trade. Protectionist forces, however, did not disappear overnight. It took a long time to reduce the overall levels of protection. In agriculture, left out of the rules of GATT, protection continued at high levels, and in the growing service sector, again left out of the GATT rules, protectionism was able to continue. Nevertheless, in terms of sentiment and of the actual reduction of protection in traded manufacturers, the period 1945–70 can be regarded as another of the relatively free-trade periods in the history of the world economy.

The slow-down in the world economy that appeared at the beginning of the 1970s and continued throughout the decade took different forms, and was of varying duration and intensity. It is often associated with the oil price rises in that decade, though it would probably be wiser to look for deeper causes. The slow-down is perhaps better accounted for by structural shifts taking place in relations between less developed and OECD countries (see Beenstock, 1983, for an interesting if debatable discussion). Whatever the explanation, the slow-down undoubtedly dates the next major shift away from free trade. The two decades since then have seen protectionism growing. Many commentators have associated the recent turn to protection with the recession of the 1970s, exacerbated by the deep and widespread depression of

1979–81. But recession alone is not enough to provide a full explanation. After all, taken in the wider perspective, Europe has become much more prosperous in the last twenty years. It has also become more protectionist in relation to the rest of the world.

In summary, across 150 years of the modern world economy there have been alternating periods of free trade and protection. Protectionism appears to have been more common, or at least sufficiently common to cause concern – though, of course, it is the magnitude that matters. Why should it have been the case, when economic theory suggests strongly that free trade is the preferable policy?

Chapter 3

A framework for the discussion

Facts do not tell their own story. 'Letting the facts speak for themselves' is an empty cliché. Facts need to be evaluated in the light of theory. Werner Sombart expressed it neatly when he wrote, 'Facts are like beads: they require a string to hold them together, to connect them. But if there is no string, no unifying idea, then even the most distinguished authorities cannot help producing unsatisfactory work' (1929, p. 5). Many economic historians accept this claim wholeheartedly and have become accustomed to employing explicit models in their work. Disagreements may arise over this approach, but there is no escaping that theory is necessary at some level. Here we make it explicit, setting out very briefly the basics of trade theory and of the explanation for protection. In practice it is only the basic theory that can ever be applied. Advanced theory seldom if ever has all, or even any of, the empirical counterparts required for testing. Basic theory is what is needed to capture the essence of the issue.

Trade theory

International trade theory demonstrates elegantly that under certain conditions (which have commonly been approximated in the real world) free trade raises welfare – improves the standard of living. Findlay recently called the free-trade argument 'the deepest and most beautiful in all of economics' (1987). Not only will individual countries adopting free trade raise their welfare but the welfare of the whole world is raised. Countries will be better-off if they exploit the comparative advantage in production they enjoy over at least some other countries. Almost all economists hold this view, which was set out most clearly by Ricardo nearly two centuries ago. The simplest demonstration of the theory is usually presented in partial equilibrium terms, showing two countries and two products. When the two domestic price ratios differ, a move from autarky to trade results in an improved allocation of resources and increased welfare.

There have been objections to the basic theory, and some refinements have been suggested. For example, there is the view that infant industries cannot reach their potential when faced with tough international competition from well established industries in 'older' countries. The argument is that the infants need to grow behind a protective wall before they are able to reach their low cost points. Another possibility is that a large country could exploit its size by imposing some of the burden of a tariff on its supplier and so benefit from what is called the 'optimal tariff'. That is, the terms of trade can be altered to the advantage of the country imposing the tariff more than enough to offset the welfare loss it would incur. A country is large in this context when it has monopoly power in all its products or in any particular product. Thus, for example, a country such as the Netherlands would not be ruled out as a contender. In the real world such large countries are very difficult to find. These points and others have been considered in the international trade literature, and they all turn out to have either a fairly insignificant impact on the prescriptions of the basic theory, or at least to have better alternative solutions than protection.

New trade theory

Some recent developments in international trade theory have focused attention on relaxing the assumption of perfect competition and on examining the consequences of economies of scale and increasing returns. This line of enquiry examines the interactions between firms as a result of oligopoly. It has been shown that in some circumstances free trade may not be the optimal policy stance, though at the same time it is not clear what exactly the nature of intervention should be.

A central aspect of these developments relates to the possibility of profit-shifting. Since oligopolies make super-normal profits, some tax is required to deliver a price that more closely approximates the perfectly competitive ideal. If the oligopoly is foreign the opportunity exists for imposing a tax that shifts at least some of the super-normal profits to the tax-imposing country. In the words of Corden the proponents of this theory 'introduce the idea that government policies such as export subsidies, or tariffs, may shift profits from a foreign firm to its domestic competitor, and that this may yield a national gain . . .' (1990).

There is not room here, nor is it the place, to go into the arguments of the new trade theory in detail. Suffice it to say that the reader can be assured that for all practical purposes the 'new' developments do not really alter the basic policy prescription – free trade is still the only sensible and manageable course to follow. Bhagwati sums up:

> The practical application of the new and theoretically valid increasing-returns-based argument for policy intervention to shift profits towards oneself in oligopolistic industries is, therefore, beset with difficulties. These are further compounded, as was the classical theoretical prescription for an optimal tariff, by the fact that the new case for export subsidization or import tariffs is based on considerations of *national* advantage and presupposes that foreign governments do not retaliate. [1988, pp. 107–8]

This is a particularly pertinent criticism, since retaliation has been such a common feature of commercial policy in history. No sooner has one country adopted a tariff than others have adopted one too, for no better reason than that the first country has done so. Talk of retaliation is again prevalent in the current protectionist climate, irrespective of the products discussed. But retaliation is even more likely today, given the products that are at the centre of discussions. To quote Bhagwati again, 'retaliation is likely in precisely the knowledge-intensive, high-technology industries in which economies of scale are presumed to be significant' (p. 108).

> The retaliatory policies provoked by attempts at profit-shifting are likely to leave each country worse off, especially if such actions spill over into other areas of trade policy or drag other players into the game simply because of the multilateral aspects of international trade. [p. 109]

The origins of many of the new developments in trade theory lie in a paper by Brander and Spencer (1981). But it really should be stressed that these authors have themselves rejected the use to which their arguments have been put:

> . . . it should be emphasised that our arguments should not be taken as support for using tariffs. The highly tariff-ridden world that would result from each country maximising

> domestic welfare taking the policies of other countries as given would be a poor outcome. Our analysis is meant to contribute to an understanding of the motives that might underlie tariff policy and provides support for the multilateral approach to trade liberalisation. [1984, p. 204]

A leading exponent of the new theory, Paul Krugman, has concluded that free trade's status 'has shifted from optimal to reasonable rule of thumb' (1987, p. 132). He nevertheless goes on to conclude that:'

> It is possible then to believe that comparative advantage is an incomplete model of trade and to believe that free trade is nevertheless the right policy. In fact this is the position taken by most of the new trade theorists themselves. [1987, p. 143]

Lobbying

If free trade is demonstrably such a good thing, why has there always been, and why is there still, so much protection about? The beginning of an explanation is contained in the basic trade theory which demonstrates that some groups in the community benefit from free trade and others lose. The obverse obviously holds – the introduction of protection benefits some at the expense of others. When the prospective beneficiaries are producers, who are invariably 'concentrated' and therefore better able to organise, they will seek to reverse free-trade policies.

There is an obvious application of this to anyone familiar with the basic two-sector trade model. The Heckscher–Ohlin model is still the dominant basic model in international trade theory. According to Heckscher–Ohlin, comparative advantage (the key concept) derives from relative factor endowment. That is, a country that has a relative abundance of a factor such as capital or labour (relative to another country) will specialise, though not necessarily completely, in the production of the goods that use that factor intensively. And it will export such goods. A country that is relatively capital-abundant will export capital-intensive goods. (Empirical tests of this proposition ran into difficulties that go under the name of the Leontif paradox. But most of the difficulties have been explained and resolved, and when the factors are specified carefully the Heckscher–Ohlin model is still found to explain basic trade patterns.)

When trade is opened up, then, after a period of no trade, in a country that is relatively labour-abundant, there will be gains for labour, and other factors will lose. This comes about since there is a move into producing goods using more labour, and the returns to labour are therefore bidded up. The returns to other factors fall. Landowners, capitalists and workers will be beneficiaries or losers according to the relative factor endowment of the country. (The country as a whole will be better-off as a result of trade.)

The issue, however, will seldom be clear-cut. There is likely to be an overlap of interests among factors. But the basic theory helps in understanding the movements into and out of free trade. Movements towards free trade are unlikely to have been the simple product of a great idea which demonstrated that the world as a whole or even the nation as a whole would be better-off. More likely they will have been a result of the beneficiaries of free trade acquiring sufficient political power or influence to bring them about. Equally a shift in the other direction will undoubtedly be associated with the political strength of those holding the opposite view.

The likelihood, then, is that free trade will be allowed to break through when the abundant factor gains sufficient political power or influence. The world, as will constantly be remarked, is more complicated than the two-sector model. Nevertheless, the basic model provides a powerful insight and is at least the starting point of any investigation.

Interest groups

The question of interest has long featured in economic discussion. The early modern discussion of interest, while never strictly defined, was centred on the interest of the individual. The notion of individual self-interest in material gain predominated. Adam Smith made this position acceptable in, for example, his remarks on the butcher and baker supplying consumers not out of benevolence but rather from self-interest. A problem with this stance was that it was not long before groups rather than individuals adopted the concept and it seemed entirely understandable and reasonable to see groups as behaving acceptably when pursuing their own interests.

The formal treatment of interest group behaviour began to attract attention in the 1960s and 1970s in what came to be called the economics of 'public choice'. This approach pursues the analysis of the costs and benefits of certain policies to different groups, and the profitability or otherwise for these groups of lobbying for or against the policy. One way of trying to explain why there is and has been so much protection is by recourse to the theory of public choice.

The basic theory of trade outlined above has shown that there are gainers and losers from protection. The gainers are generally to be found among producers. Governments, too, gain by raising revenue when imposing a tariff. Consumers are the losers from having to pay higher prices. In the language of economics there will therefore be a demand for protection and a supply. It had long been appreciated that pressure groups could buy the policies that they perceived to be to their advantage, though not by the early advocates of free trade. As Lionel Robbins put it, the free-trade prescriptions of the classical economists 'were based on a gross underestimate of the strength of producer interests in shaping the economic policy of governments.' (1976, p. 64)

The gainers, then, generate the demand for protection and the government is the source of the supply. The views of non-gainers can be influential, but generally consumers are too scattered to organise resistance in an efficient and profitable way. Producers, on the other hand, have a clear incentive to lobby, though of course that is not a costless exercise either.

But the likelihood is that there will always be good grounds for a process of exchange between government and organised interests. The government will provide tariff legislation in exchange for some form of support – financial or electoral. Because any trade regime is a public good there will always be a free-rider problem, but that is a minor complication which need not detain us in this discussion. To put it boldly, as a monopoly producer of legislation the government will face a demand curve that is an expression of the payments it will be offered. And it will have cost curves that are the sum of the forgone costs of depriving another group in some ways – either by lessening protection or providing free trade – plus the actual cost of legislation. The government will maximise gains by delivering a certain amount of protective legislation at a price that is the outcome of the intersection of these marginal cost and marginal revenue curves.

This, of course, is to simplify greatly. Before any exchange is considered some further difficulties need to be alluded to. Any bargain struck between government and lobbyist will be the outcome of pressure and resistance to it, which means that we are dealing with that very elusive concept, power. What needs to be considered is relative strength. Producers may buy protection cheaply from a weak government. But how can the relative strength of the respective participants be measured? There is always the danger of circularity. Legislation was passed, therefore the producers were stronger. But if there were no legislation, would it be because of strong government, weak pressure groups, or the absence of demand? One approach is to assume that government strength is constant and to use the degree of concentration in an industry as a proxy for the political clout of that industry. This, of course, is again a gross simplification, and in any case is valid only if the highly concentrated industries face foreign competition.

One modification that could be considered is a situation where it might be expected that producers would have greater success with a sympathetic government in power. That is, the political ideology of the government needs to be considered. There is a major objection to this, for it is not clear what a producer-sympathetic government's political colour would be. There are fashions in policy as there are in other walks of life. For example, in the 1920s the Labour Party was the party of free trade, while in the 1970s it had become protectionist. The Conservatives have changed from being overtly protectionist to espousing free trade over the same period.

In addition to the political colour of the government it would also be advisable to take into account the source of the government's power. There could be a producer-sympathetic government whose power base was the rural community. The expectation would then be that agricultural protection would rise relative to any other form.

This line of discussion leads on to another interesting but more difficult question: is it ideas that rule the world, or is it interest groups? Ideas can have subtly shifting emphasis over time, and interest is not always unambiguously defined. Nineteenth-century English landowners are an obvious example of a group that had diverse interests. In their case, land, industrial interests and urban interests were all inextricably mixed. And caution is undoubtedly called for in dealing with 'interests'. As Hume wrote, 'Though men may be much governed by interest, yet even interest itself, and all human affairs, are entirely governed by opinion.'

Ideas

The principal alternative, or more often complementary (though sometimes seen as supplementary), explanation for policy choices is the power of ideas – good or bad ideas. The case for combining the influence of interest groups with that of ideas was put most lucidly and cogently by David Henderson in his 1985 Reith Lectures. He wrote:

> However, the activity of pressure groups is not the only factor involved: if it were, trade policies would now be, and would always have been, highly and unvaryingly interventionist. To influence events, the lobbies usually have to persuade others, who do not themselves gain from what is proposed, that their cause has merit. . . . It is when pressure groups can draw support from widely accepted economic ideas, which as I have stressed need not be those of economists, that their campaigns are most likely to achieve results. [1986, pp. 63, 64]

Henderson's argument is that there are some deep-rooted 'pre-economic' ideas that play an influential role in shaping policy. One of these ideas that has been long running is that of fairness – the need to avoid social disruption from foreign competition. It is an idea that economics does not have much room for. More important, though, is the traditional mercantilist idea that any job saved by import restrictions adds to the total of employment. And to this can be added the force of economic nationalism. The combination of these ideas can be found all over the world at most times and Henderson argues that it has proved a powerful cocktail, and something that is necessary in explaining pressure-group success.

It can also be useful in helping to resolve the paradox we suggested at the outset: why have we seen the promotion of domestic competition going hand in hand with increasing international protectionist measures in the OECD countries in recent decades? Henderson sets out his argument in a more recent paper which is worth quoting at length:

> This divergence cannot be explained by either poor economic performance or the growing influence of sectional interests. If it was the unfavourable macroeconomic climate that caused governments to use protectionist devices to restrict competition from abroad, why did it not equally deter them from measures which had the intention and effect of increasing competition at home? Again, if it is held that the protectionist instruments of the 1980s were the natural resort of governments which were prisoners of interest groups, or which were concerned above all to use the power and resources of the state as a means of dispensing favours, how is it that these same governments took effective measures to restrain public expenditure, to privatise public enterprises, and to reduce the scope of official regulation of domestic transactions? . . . In order to account for the recent dualism in the OECD economies, and more generally for the prevalence of trade interventionism over a wider area and a longer period, it is necessary to bring in a third factor, namely the power of

> ideas. . . . Economic policies in general and trade policies in particular are influenced, now as in the past, by an alternative conception of how economic systems function and how economic objectives are to be defined. This conception is intuitive and timeless: it bears little relation to orthodox professional ways of thinking. In relation to trade issues it is staunchly nationalist and merchantilist, while it is apt to focus on partial and short-run rather than system-wide effects. It is this body of economic ideas, *as well as* the impact of pressure groups, which lends impetus to trade interventionism. Interventionist trade regimes themselves, and the arguments which are used to justify them, bear witness not only to the influence of well-functioning lobbies but also to the power of what I have termed do-it-yourself-economics (DIYE). [1991, pp. 28, 29]

These arguments are very persuasive and need to be held in view throughout this discussion.

If it is ideas that predominate, then they can clearly take a very long time to become accepted. For example, if in this discussion we take Adam Smith's *Wealth of Nations* as the origin of the case for freedom and specialisation in production, and as the birth of the idea of free trade, then it took more than half a century to be accepted in its home country – and then it was later rejected. And it took much longer to gain acceptance in most other countries.

It would clearly be difficult to try to determine what the relative strengths of ideas were against the competing power of interest groups. If an idea such as free trade did not get accepted it may have been that the alternative case of protection was presented more elegantly and carried the day.

Measuring protection

One of the serious problems in this exercise has been to

measure the degree of protection. It is still a problem today. The simplest approach is to take the average of the *ad valorem* tariffs, but there are difficulties. One is that these do not allow for different economic structures. Any attempt at weighting raising problems over what the weighting should be based on, and the availability of these kinds of data. A simple averaging of rates could give a misleading picture. The usual alternative is to use the total duties collected as a percentage of total imports. (Visible imports are often among the most reliable economic data that are available.) This gives a reasonable indication of the extent of protection – even if it fails to take account of a prohibitively high tariff, since in that case no duty would be collected – but in general terms in the context of the nineteenth century it turns out to be useful. Another justification for it is that in the nineteenth century many tariffs were specific (i.e. £/ton) and would require conversion to an *ad valorem* equivalent before any averaging could be done. That problem is avoided when using the duties/imports ratio.

Tariff structures in the late nineteenth century were often complex, with differential duties, and protection was further complicated by trade agreements. Thus the ratio can serve as only a rough approximation, but it is the best indicator available of the overall state of protection. Further, since it can be calculated on an annual basis, it is possible to chart its course over quite a long period and note its trend and sometimes the fluctuations around the trend.

Chapter 4

Nineteenth-century protectionism

In the course of the nineteenth century the modern world economy evolved. Following the Napoleonic Wars at the beginning of the century, Britain emerged as a powerful and increasingly industrial country and adopted free trade in the 1840s. Other countries were encouraged to follow and there was a period, as outlined above, of trade liberalisation. Then there was a collapse into protectionism. This chapter outlines the nature of the experience.

The general case for interest groups being a powerful explanatory factor in shaping commercial policies has been set out already. There are many specific studies of interest groups in different countries at different times, and they are undoubtedly useful in helping to explain the pattern of commercial policy that emerged in the course of the nineteenth century. Interest groups were influential in Britain in the first half of the century in the implementation of free trade, and equally so in Germany in the implementation of protectionism. But there were other complementing factors at work, and two of the most obvious that require some consideration are war and recession.

Free trade emerged slowly after the long period in which mercantilist philosophy had dominated economic thought in the seventeenth and eighteenth centuries. Protectionism should not be regarded as perfectly synonymous with mercantilism, though, since, to cite just one instance, protection arose quite quickly and sharply in the 1690s as a consequence of the desperate cash needs of government, 'revealing the influence of neither economists' theories nor ministers' long-term commercial policies, but simply of urgent fiscal needs' (Davis, 1966, p. 306). The writings of the classical economists, in particular Smith and Ricardo, together with an opportunist case for British exports, helped to turn the tide at the beginning of the nineteenth century.

Kindleberger has suggested that the rise of free trade in Europe owed much to the British influence, and regards it as part of a general response to the breakdown of the manor and guild system and with quite widespread concern with the promotion of exports. Export taxes had once been common – sometimes on machinery. (On the interesting question of machinery in the nineteenth century it is of interest to bear in mind that trade theory demands the removal of all restrictions. British textile manufacturers were enthusiastic free-traders so long as they had a virtual monopoly and could therefore delay the rise of foreign competition by promoting free trade in cotton goods, but they were intent on looking after their own interests. They were opposed to the export of textile machinery on the grounds that it would weaken their monopoly. Thus cotton manufacturers and mercantile interests were on opposing sides of the debate.) Export taxes were more often levied on goods which were inputs in domestic production. Different countries had different experiences but in both France and Germany the exporting interests were powerful enough to make the case successfully for the removal of export taxes. But in the end it was 'Manchester' interests and the political economists that persuaded Britain, and Britain persuaded Europe by precept and example.

In the supposed high tide of *laissez-faire* there were many powerful competing forces; interest played its part and state intervention in some form or other was never far away. Free trade was in part the product of interest, but even more so was the drift back to protection in the late nineteenth century. In the 1870s some exporting interests in Europe suffered changing fortunes. These interests had been instrumental in the introduction of free trade to Europe in the 1850s, and the changes they suffered undoubtedly lay behind the widespread reversal of free-trade policies that came in the 1870s. The root cause was the arrival of New World grain on European markets from the 1870s onwards and the harm it did to agrarian interests, which were still politically powerful.

The comparative decline of free trade in Europe in the late nineteenth century has naturally occasioned a great deal of research. Of great importance in this is the work of Gerschenkron. The proposition he advances is a challenging one – no less than that if Germany had fully embraced free trade in the mid-nineteenth century it would probably not have turned out the militaristic power that it did in the twentieth century. His thesis is that the large farmers East of the Elbe (the Junkers) were powerful enough in the middle of the century to secure protection for agriculture and to strengthen their position further. Their reactionary feudal role and persistent political influence were the major impediment to liberal democracy in Germany. Prussian power had been built up in the eighteenth century and in the process landlords had gained increasing control over their tenants. The Junkers had emerged with disproportionate political power, and that was what lay behind the introduction of the tariff: to save their grain production when the New World was opening up. Although there were many groups aligned against them the Junkers were powerful enough to carry the day – thought it did require them to form an alliance with industry.

These pressures were widespread, and they were instrumental in bringing about shifts in mood, and in preparing the way for the introduction of protection, though they may have taken a long time from conception to legislation. There is an associated element of the explanation that has often been said to trigger the implementation of protection, and that is recession. Falling profits, prices and output and rising unemployment provide the ideal stimulus to look for culprits abroad, and governments can win domestic favour more easily by extending protection in these conditions.

The impact of economics on politics is something that the 'new' political scientists have been turning their attention to. One example is the specific attempt by Gallarotti (1985) at testing the connection between economic recession and tariffs in the nineteenth century. Using some of the arguments outlined above, he examines three countries: Germany 1853–1914, the United States 1800–1914 and the United Kingdom 1800–1914. Gallarotti's interest is in the influence of the business cycle on tariff legislation, and his test is the degree of correlation between years of expansion and changes in such legislation. The actual technique is to divide the periods into quinquennia, take the average number of years of expansion and contraction within each quinquennium and associate that with the major tariff changes that took place. He claims to find a degree of association between contractionary phases in the business cycle and legislation increasing protection. As may be imagined, the test is a little tangled and the results are at best weak.

The most reliable guide to business cycle chronology for France and Germany is to be found in Burns and Mitchell (1946). Superimposing the major protectionist Acts on that chronology provides no unambiguous picture. The first important French Act came in 1885, three years after a peak in the business cycle and two years before the next trough; the comprehensive Meline tariff was introduced in 1892, two years after a peak. The German figures for tariffs and growth follow the hypothesis a little more closely but still not very convincingly.

We might not expect to find a very close association between the business cycle and tariff legislation but it is difficult to believe that the broad movements in tariff policy throughout the world in the late nineteenth century, and possibly later, have not been connected with longer-term trends in performance. The general impression gained is that periods of prosperity have promoted free trade, while long periods of depression have encouraged protection. There is certainly a close association over the longer run between prosperity and free trade.

Figures 1 and 2 (reproduced from Lindert) show the picture for the United States, the United Kingdom and Canada for 180 years, 180 years and 100 years respectively. Upon a casual examination of these figures the only strong statement that can be made on the issue is that there is no direct relationship running from economic performance to policy. Taking the United Kingdom first, what we see is the long decline in protectionist measures from mercantilism through to *laissez-faire*. From 1840 to 1920 there is no significant rise in protection (despite considerable and frequent recessions – a business cycle of clear and regular perodicity and, many would argue, periods of secular decline). Indeed, the trend from 1860

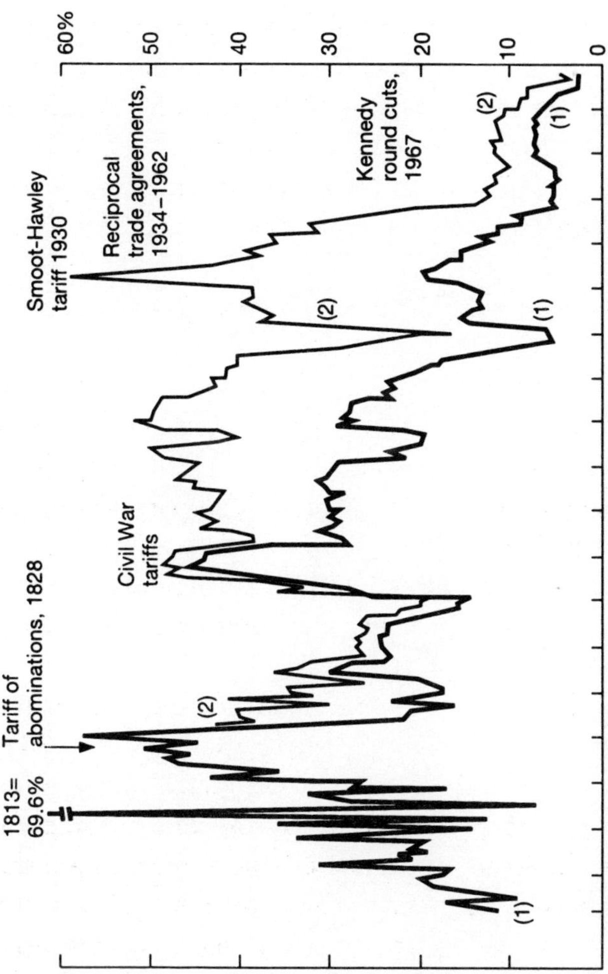

Figure 1 Average US import duties, 1792–1978 (from Lindert, 1991, fig. 13.2). Average import duty = customs revenue ÷ net imports. *Note.* (1) Duties as a percentage of all net imports. (2) Duties as a percentage of dutiable imports only. *Sources:* US Bureau of the Census, *Historical Statistics of the United States: Colonial Times to 1970*, Government Printing Office, Washington, D.C., 1976, series U193, U211, U212, Y353; *id.*, *Statistical Abstract of the United States, 1975*, Government Printing Office, Washington, D.C., 1975, table 1370

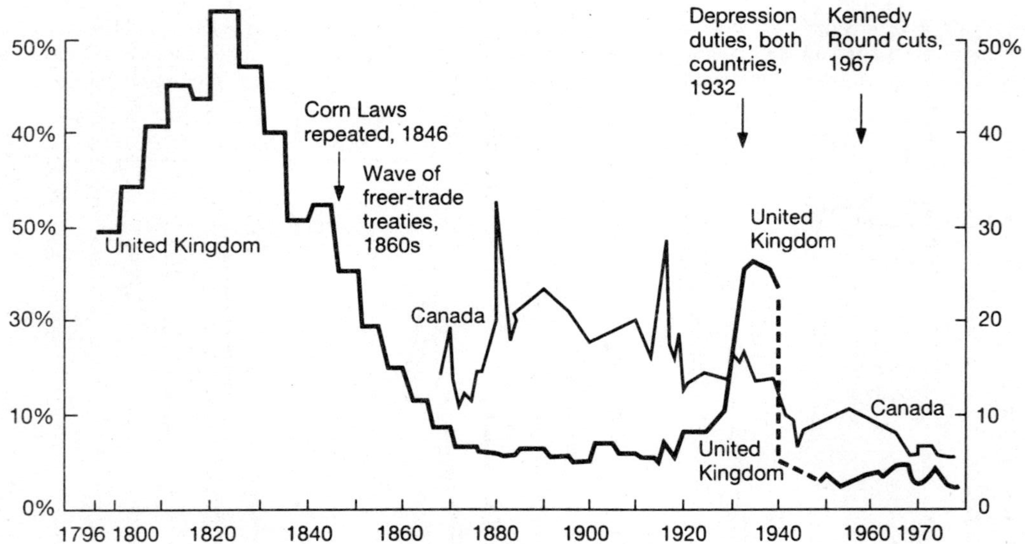

Figure 2 Average import duties, UK 1796–1979 and Canada 1868–1975, selected years; duties as a percentage of all net imports (from Lindert, 1991, fig. 13.3). Average import duty = customs revenue ÷ net imports. *Sources:* UK: A. H. Imlah, *Economic Elements of the Pax Britannica*, Harvard University Press, Cambridge, Mass., 1958, pp. 121, 160; B. R. Mitchell and P. Deane, *Abstract of British Historical Statistics*, Cambridge University Press, Cambridge, 1965, pp. 284, 394, 395; Central Statistical Office, *Annual Abstract of Statistics*, recent years. The series ending in 1938 includes non-protective customs duties on products not produced at all in Britain (e.g. tobacco, petroleum), while that beginning with 1938 is confined to protective and balance-of-payments import duties. Canada: M. C. Urquhart and K. A. H. Buckley, *Historical Statistics of Canada*, Macmillan, Toronto, 1965, pp. 173, 197, 198; Statistics Canada, *Canada Year Book*, Information Canada, Ottawa, various years. Some of the ratios for the UK and Canada compare fiscal-year customs revenue with calendar-year imports

to 1970 is clearly downwards at a low level and without variation, except of course for the striking inter-war behaviour that Lindert has labelled 'Depression duties'. I want to take issue with that in the next chapter, but, leaving that episode aside for the moment, there is no obvious support for a relationship between protection and recession in Britain. Much the same is true of Canada, even if the fall is more erratic.

The US figure is much more complicated. The United States has clearly been a much more protectionist country. There is some hint of cyclicality in the US data, particularly between 1865 and 1905, which may warrant closer examination but the most striking feature is the rather violent rushes into and out of high duties. Once again, though dismissing for the moment the leap in 1922 and 1930 (the latter has, after all, frequently been cited as the cause of the depression rather than a consequence), the US experience can be seen as one of high tariffs brought about by wars but with the *trend* being sharply downward from 1900 to 1970. By that date the United States had come into line with other countries.

At any rate, using the experience of these three English-speaking countries as a superficial test surely leads to a rejection of the hypothesis that protectionism is born in depression, or even in secular decline. What of depression and protectionist trade policies in Europe in the second half of the nineteenth century? Two features are well known. The first is that the late nineteenth century saw a growth of protectionist sentiment and of protectionist measures; and the second is that the period 1873–96 is frequently characterised as the Great Depression. Is there a relationship between the two?

First the depression. There is no doubt that the 1870s were a decade of low growth. The worse years were usually 1873–79 but some countries suffered into the 1880s. Table 1 shows the

Table 1 Income growth in European countries, 1860–1910 (% per decade)

Country	1860s (a)	1860s (b)	1870s (a)	1870s (b)	1880s (a)	1880s (b)	1890 (a)	1890 (b)	(1900–10) (a)	(1900–10) (b)
Great Britain		12·4		8·3		15·4		12.3		2.6
Germany	28·5	20.3	18.3	4.0	34.6	21.0	36.0	19.0	31.1	10.3
France	22·9	19·6	18·0	6·2	10·5	11·0	17·6	17·3	20·0	12·6
Italy	6·6	3·5	10·8	0·0	13·1	0·0	11·4	7·7	16·0	9·2
Russia		6·8		0·0	16·0	9·1	68·5	23·9	31·3	16·4
Austria				24·7		19·4		11·4		8·4
Netherlands				19·6		8·6		9·4		13·3

Source: (a) from Mitchell (1987); total growth of GDP (b) calculated from Crafts (1983). *Per capita* growth (c) from Falkus (1972).

rates of growth of total and *per capita* income across the years 1860–1914 and there is no doubt about the severity of the depression experienced in the 1870s. The story that is commonly told is of an intensive boom in the very early 1870s relating particularly to capital goods industries and that there followed around the world a long period (sometimes said to be twenty years or so) of depression. The period has attracted a lot of attention, with a variety of explanations (both monetary and real) being put forward for the long deflation – for it was primarily a long downswing in prices. Kondratieff's long swing was essentially a price cycle.

Most economic historians would deny the existence of such a prolonged depression in *output* (see, for example, Saul, 1969). Saul dealt explicitly with Britain but even if his story has wider application there are two types of resolution. First, if there was indeed no great depression in Britain, then that could be construed as support of a kind for the tariff/recession hypothesis, for neither was there any increase in protection, even though there were certainly increased grumblings about the need for it. On the other hand if the myth of depression was widespread and sufficiently strongly held it could be argued that myths are nevertheless powerful and that what matters is the perception of producers and other participants at the time. As is often the case in historical explanation it is a matter of careful interpretation and judgement.

One of the *real* (i.e. as opposed to monetary) explanations for depression in Europe is the vast amounts of US and other New World grain were landed in European countries in the 1870s following the extension of the prairie in North America and the transport revolution. With the United States maintaining high tariffs on manufactured goods, Europe was plunged into a deflationary spiral. Given the nature of this two-pronged 'attack', European industry and agriculture joined together – the alliance of 'rye and iron' – to seek tariff and non-tariff protection.

There certainly was some turn-round in policy following the gains of free trade so recently achieved in the 1850s, 1860s and early 1870s. As was noted above, in Germany the large landowners east of the Elbe had been large exporters of grain and were then strongly free-trade, but by the later 1870s their position had changed dramatically in the face of cheap imports. Pollard summarised it as 'salvation by tariff protection for whichever home interest was powerful enough to be able to secure it' (1981, p. 257). In 1879 the Germans put duties on iron and steel. In 1885 and 1887 industrial and agricultural duties were both raised. The French raised agricultural duties in 1885, and in 1887 too, and in 1892 they introduced the comprehensive Meline tariff. The Austro-Hungarians' tariffs were still moderate in 1878 but were raised in 1882 and 1887. The Italians, who had low rates in 1878, introduced a high general tariff in 1887 and raised them higher in 1894. In addition there was a breakdown of 'most favoured nation' treatment and tariff wars broke out in Europe, notably between the French and the Italians, and between the Russians and the Germans.

All this meant that between 1875 and 1895 duties on manufactured articles in Europe as a whole rose. There were attempts, such as that in 1891 by the new German chancellor, Caprivi, to reverse the process. But the general trend was towards intensification, so that by 1913 the average levels of tariffs in Europe ranged from 10 per cent to 40 per cent, with the Germans at the lower end of the range, the French around 20 per cent and Russians and Spanish at the top. When the major pieces of legislation are superimposed on the graphs of output there is some evidence for the case that several years of hardship were followed by protectionist policies in many countries.

Economic historians are justifiably cautious about reading the pattern of events from the statute book, and tariff legislation is no exception. It did not necessarily translate into corresponding duties. The legislation should be contrasted with the actual protection provided, as captured in the ratio of duties to imports. This measure reveals relatively little change across the period. The direction is unmistakably upward but its extent is not always large. French duties moved from 5 per cent to 8 per cent by this measure; German duties from 6 per cent to 8 per cent, Italian ones from 8 per cent to 10 per cent. The British ratio rose very slightly, as can be seen from Figure 1.

There are perhaps two reasons for this. The first is that the protectionist turn-round observed in continental Europe was not found in Britain, possibly because the British were not subject to the same pressures from agriculture. The second is that the British clearly had more opportunities of escape from depression through labour migration. But why did the other European countries adopt protection on this occasion and not during previous deep recessions? It may be that the answer depends on another element in the story, and that is that the degree of concentration (i.e. the proxy for political clout) had changed. It may be that the scale of enterprise had something to do with it. This was certainly a period of 'combination', of great growth in firm size. It is Pollard's conclusion that the industry successful in getting aid was usually highly concentrated; that local deputies and representatives were mobilised, and firms' resources set aside for propaganda and agitation. There was a further factor in Europe, too: the agrarian interest still had more political power than its economic contribution warranted. All this satisfies in a loose way the hypotheses advanced above, but the special features should be borne in mind.

In summary, in Europe in the second half of the nineteenth century protectionist measures increased. They came mostly in the 1880s and 1890s. And while there may not have been so great a depression as formerly characterised the period, the 1870s and 1880s do seem to have been a particularly deep and prolonged downswing. A greatly reduced agricultural sector, together with migration, may have helped Britain escape the consequences of protectionist pressure but other Europeans were not so well placed. There the increasing size of the industry and increasing concentration were probably important, together with the disproportionate political power of agricultural interests.

Chapter 5

The impact of protection in the nineteenth century

What impact did protection have in the late nineteenth century? Did it improve the economic performance of the countries where it was introduced? Did countries with protectionist trade policies have faster rates of economic growth than they would otherwise have had, and faster than those of non-protectionist countries? These questions are not easily answered, but the accumulating evidence suggests that the impact was small, weak and possibly even perverse. The immense difficulties in trying to estimate the effects of the tariff should always be recognised. The eminent contemporary economist Taussig wrote, 'The economic effects of [tariffs] it is impossible to follow empirically . . . more baffling is the task of following or measuring their effects on general prosperity.' (1921, p. 539). No great advances have been made since.

That has not prevented assertions being made about the impact of protection on countries' economic performance. For example, one of the earliest historians of the tariff, W. Ashley, wrote of America: '. . . in 1842 there began a revival in trade and commerce . . . it is probable that it was quickened by the increased protection' (1910, p. 215). While he is referring to cyclical recovery, Ashley generally favoured interventionist policies. Those who are opposed to them tend to conclude unfavourably on the policies. Imlah, for instance, wrote about 'The success of free trade' and 'The failure of protection' (1958).

Since these early attempts at assessment there has been a lot of work on individual countries based on greatly improved data. These studies do allow some slightly finer judgements to be arrived at. Before turning to them some comment is necessary on the problems of measuring the extent of protection.

Tariffs and economic growth

This section sets out some of the types of evidence available on the issue of protection and economic growth. That evidence ranges from what can only be called casual observation at one end of the scale to some more rigorous regression analysis, the changing degree of openness in economies, the possibility of the optimal tariff, and finally to some suggestions as to what indications of the effective rate of protection can reveal.

One attempt at establishing the relationship between protection and growth was that of Bairoch (1972). Bairoch did not use data on protection but simply classified some European countries (France, Germany and Italy) as being either 'free-trade' or 'protectionist' in different periods. The free-trade periods for each of these countries were respectively: 1860–90, 1862–79 and 1863–87. He compared their growth rates in those periods with growth before and after, in what, by definition, were protectionist periods. The trouble with this is that commercial policy is seen as being either switched on or switched off, when in fact it is continuum. Bairoch's study cannot take account of varying degrees of protection. He nevertheless felt able to conclude very strongly that liberalising trade was harmful. For example, of France he stated, 'The liberalisation of trade substantially slowed down economic growth . . . the reintroduction of protectionism led to acceleration in the rate of economic growth.' (p. 221).

In fact it is possible to be much more precise than Bairoch. As a first step the growth of GDP and industrial production by decade, together with average tariff levels, can be compared more carefully. Table 2 sets out the data for seven countries for as much of the century as there are data for. It would be impossible from a comparison of these data to come to the same conclusion as Bairoch. High-growth decades often go with big reductions in tariffs. This may be so because high growth is the cause, even if with some lag, of the reduced protection.

It is also interesting to note from Table 2 that, apart from Russia, there is no great difference in the degree of protection captured in these measures for the European countries. Britain, supposedly free-trade, had a gently declining ratio of around 4 per cent. The French ratio did rise to 12 per cent in 1890 but was closer, on average, to 8. That is certainly twice the British level but it should also be remembered that Britain's was a more open economy and a comparison of GDP would narrow the difference. The German ratio was always slightly lower than the French. Even Italy, often singled out for its destructive protectionism, finishes the period not far out of line with the French.

There are annual data on these variables of protection and growth for several countries for the important forty years or so prior to the First World War. The data, it must be stressed again, are somewhat fragile. But bearing that in mind, and exercising due caution over the results, it is possible to carry out a more rigorous examination by running some regressions.

Table 2 Nominal tariff rates (*a* total duties as a percentage of exports) and economic growth (*b* per decade)

	US			*France*			*Germany*			*Italy*			*UK*			*Japan*			*Russia*		
	(a)	(b)		(a)	(b)		(a)	(b)		(a)	(b)		(a)	(b)		(a)	(b)		(a)	(b)	
Decade	Nom.	GDP	IP	Nom.	GDP	IP	Nom.	GDP	IP	Nom.	GDP	IP	Nom.	GDP	IP	Nom.	GDP	IP	Nom.	GDP	IP
1820s	46				22	4·1									36·4						
1830s	25				22·4	19·1								20·5	33·3						
1840s	24	61			17·8	30·9							34	21·6	33·3						
1850s	21	57		12	13·1	25·7		28·7	36·6				15	27·6	9·3				26		
1860s	36	28		5	22·9	3·4		28·5	46·2	8	6·6	25	8	22·9	26·8				17		25
1870s	31	60		4	18·0	19·6	6	18·3	23·8	9	10·8	7.7	5	15·9	15·6				14		50
1880s	30	47		7	10·5	5·9	8	34·6	48·1	16	13·1	8·5	5	17·3	18·3		55·2	15·7	25	16·0	45·5
1890s	24	36		8	17·6	12·6	9	36·0	48·8	15	11·4	29·8	5	21·7	25·0		65·3	285·5	34	68·5	85·3
1900s	25	52		8	20	19·8	8	31·1	45·8	10	16·0	55·7	5	10·2	6·5		11·1	53·0	30	31·3	32·3

Source: Capie (1983a). By courtesy of Macmillan Ltd, London

The hypothesis that economic growth was a function of protection can be tested. The test can be made to accommodate the plausible assumption that it was the protection of previous periods (or of the period before that, or an accumulation of weighted amounts of that of previous periods) that contributed to the current period's economic growth. (In the jargon, a polynomial distributed lag is used.) When such tests are run for Germany, Italy, the United Kingdom and Russia (the countries for which there are long enough runs of reasonably good data) we find that there is no explanation of growth to be found in protection (Capie, 1983). The statistical results of the exercise turn out to be very weak, and that should not really be surprising. Economic growth is not well understood, but by any reckoning there would be a long list of factors that would come above commercial policy in the explanation. Commercial policy is notoriously hard to police and enforce, and examples abound of the ways in which firms get round trade barriers facing their exports (Kirchner, 1981).

The extent of openness

The weakness of these regression results, together with the earlier superficial examination of the data for more countries over a longer period, certainly suggests the conclusion that protection did not improve economic performance. What other kinds of evidence can be marshalled? One possibility is import ratios – the ratio of imports to total output. If, as is usually asserted – and the evidence does support the assertion – protection was rising in the late nineteenth century and growth was improving, then import ratios should have been falling. An advantage of these ratios is that they embody all the protectionist measures contributing to changes in imports, and so overcome some of the deficiencies of the previous measure, though at the same time they are clearly the outcome of a number of other factors.

The ratios are presented in Table 3 for the seven countries that made up the great bulk of the world economy in the period. The ratios for all the countries, except the United States and the United Kingdom, are stable or rising between 1850 and 1900. (Export ratios and therefore total trade ratios were similar.) The exceptions are interesting. The United States has a falling ratio (implying less and less openness) and yet duties/imports were falling throughout the period. More interesting is the fact that the United Kingdom also has a falling trade ratio, when it was the country holding to free trade. It could be argued that other factors dominated, but the result as it stands lends more weight to the suggestion that protection was not as effective as is sometimes claimed.

However, a qualification is necessary. The ratios were calculated using current price data (in the absence of consistent constant price data). Volume data for the United Kingdom show an import ratio rising quite steeply from 19 per cent in 1870 to 28 per cent in 1913. The same is true of the United States. Lipsey (1963) showed that, using constant price data, the United States actually becomes more open, and that agrees with the protectionist measure being in decline. Thus although the United States introduced more tariff legislation (if with some small reversals before the First World War) and talked protectionist, the indication contained in the duties collected as a percentage of imports, showing relatively declining protection, is supported by the fact that the import ratio in volume terms (the better measure) was actually rising.

Great Britain

Britain also provides some other, and different kinds of,

Table 3 Trade ratios

	France		*Germany*		*Italy*		*UK*		*US*		*Japan*		*Russia*	
Decade	*M*	*X*	*M*	*X*	*M*	*X*	*M*	*X*	*M*	*X*	*M*	*X*	*M*	*X*
1840–50	4·7	5·6					18·2	14·1	8·9	5·9				
1850–60	8·7	8·3					24·9	19·5	9·8	5·6				
1860–70	9·0	9·5			9·2		30·7	23·7	9·1					
1870–80	11·6	11·8			9·3		28·0	21·6	8·5	6·2				
1880–90	14·5	13·4	17·4	15·8	10·4		28·2	21·5	8·0	6·7	5·1		6·5	
1890–1900	14·5	13·6	18·1	14·1	9·8		26·4	18·1	7·3	6·9	8·3		5·9	
1900–10	15·2	15·1	18·3	16·8	13·1		26·9	19·3	5·9	6·8	13·5		6·0	

Note: M imports, X exports.
Source: Capie (1983a). By courtesy of Macmillan Ltd, London.

evidence. The earliest accounts of British commercial policy in the nineteenth century showed that Britain had benefited greatly from adhering to the principles of free trade. In the Victorian boom years of 1850–70, immediately following the adoption of free trade, trade grew at its fastest recorded rate, by more than 4 per cent per annum, and contemporaries were satisfied that the removal of impediments to trade was responsible. But a view also developed that British policy was in some respects, at the very least, pragmatic and possibly even cynical. The emergence of the latter view derived from the fact that, as the supreme manufacturing nation by the middle of the nineteenth century, Britain simply aimed at preserving her manufacturing monopoly. Some trading nations saw British sponsorship of international free trade as a Machiavellian way of kicking down the ladder by which Britain had climbed to supremacy.

The most widely accepted view has been that the abolition of tariffs in Britain stimulated the demand for imports in Britain, which in turn stimulated the demand for British exports abroad. That version has never been entirely convincing, ignoring as it does the wider aspects of the philosophy of *laissez-faire* which dominated British life in the middle years of the century. Indeed, one study turns the cynical interpretation on its head (McCloskey, 1980).

McCloskey's view is that the elimination of duties certainly increased British demand for importables. But since this was a non-eligible portion of world demand it must have raised the word price by a non-negligible amount. That is, the terms of trade would have turned against Britain, and the deterioration in the terms of trade resulting from lowered duties could have offset the advantages of more trade and so reduced the national income. This argument of the optimal tariff concludes that in fact Britain did suffer a loss of income as a result of reducing tariffs. Specifically, the cost of free trade over the period from 1841 to 1881 was 4 per cent of national income. That is, national income was 4 per cent lower in 1881 than it would otherwise have been. The point of drawing attention to this recent challenge to accepted views is to make the point that nineteenth-century Britain was different from most other countries, and lessons should not be drawn too hastily from its experience.

To sum up, there are poor grounds for accepting a story based on available nominal tariff rates, or even on duties collected. The conventional view is weakened further by the evidence of trade ratios. The indications are that there was not a great deal of change in these ratios.

An alternative approach

The kind of evidence presented above is inclining one way – it suggests that protectionism has not been measured as well as it might have been in some of the literature, and the best measures show that it has not had the large positive impact sometimes claimed. In more recent years different approaches to measuring the tariff and making comparisons have been developed. The most important has been the level of 'effective protection'. This measure takes into account the tariff on a final product and the tariff on inputs used in that product, and expresses such a net tariff over the value added in production. It is generally accepted that where such calculations can be made they allow a better view of the scale of protection. The data requirements are greater, and unfortunately data are not always readily available. Nevertheless, using the framework of effective protection, and some informed guesses on its likely changing magnitude, together with some individual studies of effective protection, brings further evidence to the account. It all lends weight to the position that has been set out above.

In the use of effective protection two main elements are important. One is the level of nominal tariffs on inputs and the extent to which they produced a lower 'net tariff' (the numerator in the formula) and hence a lower effective rate of protection. That would have resulted in a level of protection lower than would be read either from average nominal rates or from duties collected as a proportion of import values. The second element in the calculation is the proportion that value added constituted of final output (the denominator) and how it might have changed over the course of the century.

The argument being advanced here is in two parts. The first is that the numerator was reduced as a result of tariffs on inputs. The second is that, as the value added was growing through time with increasing technological sophistication in the economy, so effective protection was diminishing. Both elements were therefore operating to reduce protection over the nineteenth century.

The nominal tariff on inputs

Taking the first element, the tariff on inputs, it is worth recounting the sources and objectives of tariffs at the beginning of the nineteenth century. Three points may be made. The first is that, in the trade regulations inspired by mercantilism in the eighteenth century, little distinction was drawn between one type of import and another. Imports were all equally undesirable and they all tended to be taxed to a similar extent. Although the mercantilist doctrine was disintegrating by the end of the eighteenth century, imports had for so long been regarded as inimical to the national economy that a legacy carried over into the nineteenth century appears to have been a strong force working to deter imports, and this regardless of the degree of manufacture they embodied.

Secondly, given the scale of the wars (European and North America) that the nineteenth century opened with, the pressure on government revenue was intense and in the days of nascent fiscal policy a favourite resort was import duties. Thus with the objective being to reduce the flow of imports and at the same time to raise revenue from as wide a range of items as possible there was little if any discrimination between tariffs on inputs and tariffs on final products. The third factor operating to produce tariffs on inputs was the political power of the landed classes in Europe, and of agricultural interests in America at this early stage of industrialisation. They were both in a position to secure tariffs on agricultural or primary products, many of which were the raw materials for manufacturing.

These three factors operating at the beginning of the nineteenth century combined to produce a strong likelihood and the actual imposition of tariffs on the raw materials and other inputs of emerging industry. In other words there were forces working to reduce the net tariff. Obviously a calculation of the degree of protection based on total duties collected as a percentage of total imports would yield a misleadingly high figure when duties on inputs were high, as compared with the better guide given by even a rough measure of effective protection. The French experience at the beginning of the nineteenth century illustrates the point. After the breakdown of the treaty with Britain in the 1780s there followed twenty years of war and economic blockade with retaliatory protection. In the peace that followed duties remained high and remained in force on raw materials. For example in the 1820s there were duties on cotton thread, leather, wool and iron bars. The *ad valorem* duty on iron was 50 per cent, and it was higher on steel; not until the last quarter of the century were the first drawbacks being granted, and they were few and tiny.

Sometimes in the early years of the century it was a combination of agricultural and manufacturing interests that secured protection. And the remarkable thing is that in the closing years of the century, although mercantilist ideas had lost their appeal (even if the period has been described as neo-mercantilist) and although a clearer awareness of something akin to the net tariff had evolved, it was the severe agricultural depression of the 1870s and 1880s that saw the agricultural sector again clamouring for protection and again linking with interested manufacturing groups. It was their combined force that contributed to the increases in nominal rates from 1880 to 1910. For example, in Germany there were no duties on raw materials in the 1860s but they were reintroduced under the tariff of 1881. Among the important products affected were timber, coal, ferro-manganese, steel wire and textile yarns. Once again, therefore, given the protection secured for raw material products in this process, nominal rates went up all round, but the effective rate of protection need not always have risen.

A factor that would have contributed to this effect was the growing fashion for specific as opposed to *ad valorem* duties at the end of the century, and the effect that price changes had on this. Proportionately the revenue from a fixed specific duty rises when the price falls. Prices were changing over the period 1870–1910 – falling from around 1870 to the late 1890s and then showing some rise through to 1914. Since the price of raw materials fell more steeply than the prices of finished goods, the equivalent *ad valorem* rates on inputs would have risen more than rates on final goods. In other words, even where there was no legislative change, protection as gauged by measures of nominal rates may have increased while the effective rate of protection actually fell.

Value added as a proportion of output

Let us turn now to the second element, the proportion of value added in gross output. The concept of effective protection was developed and refined in the 1960s and had some obvious applications to developing countries. In an age of multinationals, vertical integration and many rapidly developing economies the point was frequently made that a low value added produced high rates of effective protection. If this low value added for emerging manufacturing industry held true of the early nineteenth century it would have been a factor pulling in the opposite direction from the tariffs on inputs – low value added producing high effective rates of protection. But if it were rising thereafter, with economic development, it would have increased the relative size of the denominator and lowered effective protection.

The evidence on value added is scarce, but it would seem plausible to expect a rising ratio of value added to gross output as a consequence of industrial products becoming increasingly complex and this being a rising function of time. Some evidence for this – the tendency for the ratio to rise – has been adduced for the United States (Whitney, 1973). It is unlikely that the value added was very low in the early years of the nineteenth century or moved very significantly in the course of the century. However, as machine tools and engineering products, motor cars and chemicals developed at the close of the century the ratio was undoubtedly moving upwards and so exerted a depressing effect on the effective rate.

There were therefore two factors operating to keep effective protection down in the course of the century. What evidence there is lends support to the view that, in spite of nominal tariffs generally rising in the late nineteenth century, effective rates were constrained by the growing share of value added in gross output and the continuing tariffs on raw materials and other inputs. To these considerations should be added the small scale on which drawbacks were granted.

Studies of effective protection

Only one serious study treats these matters specifically, and even then only peripherally, but the conclusion lends further weight to the point. Of the United States in the late nineteenth and early twentieth centuries, in spite of the supposedly dramatic increase in protection from the Dingley and McKinley tariffs, Hawke says:

> there was much less increase in the protection given to U.S. industries between 1879 and 1904 than is commonly believed. The development of technology giving value added a larger share in the gross output of many industries and increased tariffs on inputs to many industries offset such increases in tariffs on industrial output as took place. [Hawke, 1975]

Hawke adds that agriculture and forestry had negative effective protection.

Hawke's (1975) study of the United States suggests also that there is no simple linear approximation to the relationship between nominal and effective rates. In the closing twenty years of the century there was not so much a general increase in protection as a rearrangement, with the most significant increases affecting wool, silk and hosiery, and the most significant decreases coming in cotton, iron and steel, and boots and shoes.

In the 1970s and 1980s some studies appeared of effective rates of protection for individual industries in a few countries in the late nineteenth century. While the results do not allow conclusions to be drawn about the relationship between effective rates and overall performance, some are suggestive, and they contain, almost without exception, support for the picture presented above. For example, in a study of the Italian engineering industry in the fifteen years before the First World War, Toniolo (1977) found that the duty on inputs of iron and steel resulted in the industry being placed at a disadvantage in respect of foreign competitors. The nominal rates in the industry were not high but the effective rates were close to zero.

In a wider study of the major industries in the German economy at the end of the nineteenth century Webb (1977) found levels of effective protection that contradicted the traditional contention that tariffs benefited all producing classes. In a later study Webb (1981) examined iron and steel, cotton textiles and agriculture over the years 1879–1914. The output of German iron and steel over these years was tremendous. Steel output grew at over 10 per cent per annum between 1879 and 1913 from an already substantial base, and pig iron output grew at over 6 per cent per annum over the same period. But the effective rate of protection, apart from a brief exceptional period, was not generally high.

Webb concluded that the tariff had little direct effect on the growth of output in this industry. The results for agriculture show that, in contrast to the more common average relationship of 2:1 between effective and nominal rates obtained for recent periods, the rates on rye and wheat were almost always close to identical. For some branches of textiles the effective rates were very high, though they were falling drastically and as the period closed one branch at least had a negative rate.

Webb did not deny that the traditional contention that tariffs fostered economic growth remained a possibility. He believed that tariffs encouraged vertical integration and probably therefore indirectly stimulated the growth of German domestic production, though probably not *per capita* income – though, as we have seen, its effect on steel output may be regarded as insignificant. He makes the important point, and one that has implications for all these studies, that the usual assumption under international trade theory of fixed quantities of productive factors does not hold in this period. The remarkable mobility of productive factors internationally meant that the pattern of effective protection alone did not determine the effect of the tariff in redistributing income. The fixity of land meant that this factor benefited most.

In another study, limited to the iron and steel industry in the United States, the results are mixed (Sundararajan, 1970). Sundararajan's figures do confirm Hawke's in that the trend of effective rates of protection on pig iron is downward after 1885–90. But while Sundararajan claimed that 'tariffs played a crucial role in the early years of the pig iron industry' (both nominal and effective rates suggested this), in the regression equations there was a negative sign on the tariff coefficient showing that output increased when tariffs decreased. This may be a dubious result, but if it could be accepted at its face value it would be support indeed for the view that tariffs impeded the progress of the industry and hindered performance.

Exchange rates

There is another point that needs to be made, and it concerns exchange rates. In 1870 only Britain of these major industrialising countries was on the gold standard. Most of Europe was on a silver or some bimetallic standard. Russia among others had the appearance of being on a metallic standard but in fact operated on a depreciated paper currency. In the course of the 1870s a fall in silver prices took place, largely as a result of the increasing American output of silver, and that in turn led to the depreciation of silver currencies. Similarly, for those with a bimetallic standard, silver replaced gold and those currencies also depreciated.

Some trading advantage (of a protectionist kind) therefore followed for those depreciating, as against gold, but the instability of exchange rates that accompanied it encouraged countries to adopt the gold standard. Germany led the way in 1871 and the others followed. France moved towards gold but still held to a form of bimetallism. The United States fixed the dollar in terms of gold in 1879 but had been operating a *de facto* gold standard for some years. Russia and Japan did not in fact adopt the gold standard until the late 1890s. The gold purchases made by the countries adopting the gold standard added to the pressure on the remaining silver currencies to such an extent that by the end of the 1870s the major industrial countries had effectively adopted the gold standard. In other words, in the closing quarter of the nineteenth century, almost coincident with the rise in protection, came widespread adoption of the gold standard, and countries that adopted it relinquished whatever flexibility they had had from the previous arrangement.

Tariff policy is non-monetary but its effect depends upon

fixed or floating exchange rates. Brunner (1976) showed that the unambiguous effect of higher tariffs with fixed exchange rates was to increase the domestic money supply and lower foreign money supply. Therefore, whatever benefits accrued from the raising of tariffs in the 1880s and 1890s to those who adopted the gold standard, there was the offsetting factor of a rising money supply raising prices and hence reducing competitiveness. The final result would represent another negative effect for the tariff.

In summary, this examination of a quite wide array of evidence on the impact of protection (very largely the tariff) in the nineteenth century points to the fact that the tariff did not have a significant economic impact on the economies in which it was introduced. Their growth performance was not enhanced; but nor does much harm appear to have been done to their individual performance. Individual industries would have been fostered in the short run and then handicapped in the long run. It is worth reiterating here, though, that there is no evidence for the assertion that countries prospered behind high protective walls.

There is one further area of explanation: that there were exogenous factors working to offset the impact of protection. If transport costs fall, for example, the impact is the same as a decrease in every affected country's tariffs. Transport costs were tumbling in the late nineteenth century with the spread of railways and the revolution in shipping. Furthermore, any change that reduces risk or the transaction costs of trade will have similar effects. It could easily be argued that the world grew more stable over the period 1880–1913.

Why, then, all the fuss? The answer surely is that the problems that arose were essentially political, if none the less serious for that. The international climate carried considerable dangers for international trade. This chapter has shown that the belief that late nineteenth-century protection was high should now be modified. The fact that no clear relationship can be found between protection and economic performance therefore becomes less surprising. Equally, there is no denying that protectionist talk and legislation went hand in hand with nationalism, and that wrecked the world economy in the war of 1914–18.

Chapter 6

Inter-war origins

The international economy after the war

The move towards protection

In the years between the two World Wars the international economy was in considerable turmoil. A variety of problems dogged the immediate post-war recovery of many countries and severely hampered the progress of international economic relations. That in turn led to further problems or at least exacerbated problems within and between countries. The principal legacy of financing the 'Great War' was differential inflation rates and price levels in 1919–20 and hence exchange rate problems. There had also been soaring domestic and international debt, and diminished resources with which to service the debt. Domestic production and international trade patterns were badly disrupted. Added to all this was the burden of reparation payments for some and the difficulties of transfer for others.

Worse, there was no agreement internationally on what needed to be done to resolve many of the problems. The United States has sometimes been found culpable for failing to take up the role of international leader that Britain had played before 1914 but was in no position to continue with after 1920. The

United States is regarded as having become isolationist after the war, regretting its involvement in what it regarded as a European problem. Whether or not that view is fair, or too simple, the United States did refuse to join the League of Nations, which was one kind of signal. It certainly declined to take up the role of international leader.

But worst of all, from the point of view of international trade, was the almost immediate adoption of new protectionist measures. Since in 1920 the United States was the biggest, richest and least war-ravaged economy in the world, these were the worst kind of signals to send to a world that urgently needed the opposite by way of example and encouragement.

In 1921 the United States introduced an Emergency Tariff Act, largely as a defensive measure against Europeans who were showing signs of increasing protection. The Emergency Act was the forerunner of the Fordney–McCumber legislation, passed in September 1922. That introduced tariffs which resulted in the average rate on dutiable imports being raised by almost 50 per cent, from 26·8 per cent (already high by international standards) to 38·2 per cent. These measures made it impossible for many debtor countries to earn the dollars they needed to repay interest on their debt.

Protection quickly developed in another group of countries, too – those that had been deprived of European manufactures during the war years. They had developed their own substitute products. When world manufacturing production began to get re-established these countries sought to protect their own new industries. Further, the creation of new states in Europe increased the tariff frontiers by some 12,000 miles as the new countries also sought to protect their own industry. Old countries were not immune. Many raised their tariffs on both industrial and agricultural goods. Primary producers, not to be left out, sought to protect their new industries, on the one hand, and, on the other, their agriculture against the deteriorating terms of trade that it faced. An element in almost all these cases was that tariffs would provide bargaining power in anticipated trade negotiations.

Such was the move to protection in the decade after the war that there were almost universal increases in tariff levels, as the figures (duties as a percentage of dutiable imports) in Table 4 show. The League of Nations was impotent in the face of such determined action by individual countries. World economic conferences were organised by the League in 1927, 1929 and 1930. They were all quite realistic in their ambitions, aiming to get rid of non-tariff barriers to trade and prevent any further increases in tariff levels. They all failed. Leaders invariably came away from the conferences mouthing high-sounding statements and all in apparent agreement with one another on the need to increase free trade. But when they returned to their countries they were unable to resist the political pressures that

Table 4 Tariff levels in 1913 and 1931 (duties as a percentage of dutiable imports)

Country	*1913*	*1931*
Germany	16·7	40·7
France	23·6	38·0
Italy	24·8	48·3
Austria	22·8	36·0
Czechoslovakia	22·8	50·0
Hungary	22·8	45·0
Spain	37·0	68·5
United States	41·0	53·0

Source: Liepman (1938, p. 415), Humphrey (1955, p. 74). Reproduced in fuller form in Conybeare (1987, p. 236).

awaited them. In 1933 at yet another world economic conference, held in London, an attempt was made to reach a tariff truce, but if failed.

The Great Depression was truly worldwide but there was a considerable range of experience. In the depression of 1929 to 1932 the British suffered only relatively mild setbacks while the American economy collapsed. Most of Europe fared badly, and so did all countries heavily reliant on the US market. Both the United States and the United Kingdom used the depression as an excuse to adopt protectionist measures. Their actions brought dismay around the world and provoked the tariff wars that accompanied the trade collapse in the following decade.

The peak of economic activity in the United States came in the middle of 1929. The country then fell into the worst economic depression in history. Gross domestic product fell by 35 per cent and unemployment soared to 14 million – 25 per cent of trade union membership. In 1929, in part because of the spread of European protection, a congressman and a senator, Hawley and Smoot respectively, proposed fresh tariff legislation and saw the Bill through that took their name as the Smoot–Hawley Act of 1930. The Americans already had high rates of duty. This Act introduced the highest rates of duty in US history, though it applied to a relatively small range of goods. Nevertheless, the Act embodied increases on 250 agricultural items, and various sectors of industry secured high increases. It was to prove an important landmark in the tariff wars that spread in the following years. It marked the breakdown of the trade negotiating system which had clung to 'most favoured nation' treatment (whatever was granted to one country had to be extended to all other countries) since the middle of the nineteenth century.

Also of significance in terms of international impact was the adoption of protection by Britain. Britain had for long been the foremost exponent of free trade and its leading exemplar. But in a series of measures at the beginning of the 1930s she reversed those policies and turned to protection. At Ottawa in August 1932 at the Empire Conference the British established other protectionist measures for agriculture. At Ottawa the motto was: Britain first, the empire second and foreigners last. Britain imposed quotas on both empire and foreign imports.

It was at this time that a great deal of discussion took place about the possibility of a customs union. There were those who were keen to establish such a union – a common tariff and no internal tariffs – in the empire. As it turned out there were too many obstacles. In the end there was a poor approximation in a range of increased imperial preference measures – reduced duties on goods coming from the empire. The kind of distortion this led to is illustrated by the American car manufacturers who moved plant across the border from Detroit into Canada to assemble cars for export to British territories.

The protectionist stance of these two leading countries in the world economy – one the largest and richest, and the other the oldest and most committed free-trader – produced dire results in the following few years. Around the world (and even across much of the United States) there was near despair at the passing of the Smoot–Hawley Act. The *New York Times* reported the view that in passing the Smoot–Hawley Act 'war was declared by the Republican Party against the rest of mankind' (11 February 1932). And equally there was dismay at the action of the British. Of course, many other countries were highly protectionist, but at the time any lead on trade liberalisation had to come from these two. When the leading economies in the world took such action it was widely regarded as further evidence of the breakdown in international trading relations.

The impact of the Smoot-Hawley Act

There is no mistaking the international impact the Smoot–Hawley tariff had. It provoked immediate and widespread recriminations and, more important, retaliatory protectionist measures. Thirty countries immediately protested against the new tariff, and many imposed countervailing tariffs within a week. The following examples give a flavour of what happened.

Italy immediately boycotted a range of American goods and raised the duties on others, including cars, car parts, radios and so on. Italy also by decree switched to other countries as a source of imports. It specified the countries that imports could be purchased from as only a dictatorship could.

The French followed suit. Indeed, to some extent they set the pace. The French Minister of Commerce, Louis Rollin, made a speech on 30th April 1931 which declared that retaliation was the current basis of French commercial policy (Bailey, 1932, p. 96). The particular approach of the French was the use of quotas, that is, the imposition of maximum quantities of goods which could be imported from specified countries. This strategy got round some of the constraints of important trade treaties that the French had signed. The first decree was issued in 1931 and many others followed, establishing quotas on a wide range of raw materials and foodstuffs. Others were introduced in 1932 on manufactured goods, and in total hundreds of items were covered.

The Germans were particularly aggrieved at the action of the Americans and the British, believing that they had been singled out for treatment. In the course of 1932 they raised their tariffs by 100 per cent and drove their imports down to the levels of 1898. There were many claims at the time that rising unemployment in Germany was a direct result of the American and British protectionist measures. While it is difficult to adduce evidence to support these claims, the economic climate contributed to Germany going down the road to a totalitarian state which regulated trade strictly, usually bilaterally, and also implemented a regimented payments system.

The Swiss believed that their watch industry had been singled out for discriminatory treatment and indeed that it was put in jeopardy as a result of the increase in American duties of 300 per cent. The Swiss therefore boycotted American products. The Spanish too took action by immediately withdrawing 'most favoured nation' treatment. When tariffs were insufficient to stem the flow of imports, countries followed the French example and turned to quotas. Sixteen European countries were using quotas on a wide range of products by the middle of the 1930s.

The resentment aroused by the Smoot-Hawley tariff extended well beyond Europe. Tariff revisions followed immediately in Canada, Cuba, Mexico, Australia, New Zealand and other countries. The Canadian case is of particular interest. The Americans' closest and biggest customer was taxed like any other. Most of Canada's primary output had duties raised against it. In return the Canadians raised duties massively on US goods and just for good measure lowered them on British goods. The Japanese economy was emerging in the 1920s as a significant trading power. Japanese exports more than doubled in value between 1920 and 1939. Japan too raised its tariffs in response to the American action.

Some have viewed the British adoption of protection in

1931 and 1932 as yet another response to the Americans. But it is more sensible to see it as the triumph of a particular lobby which had been working away for some time (admittedly in a highly protectionist world environment) and which was almost certain of eventual success even before Smoot–Hawley was enacted. However, it certainly was not hampered by the American action. There were many other tariff increases around the world in 1929 and 1930 which have also been seen as retaliation against Smoot–Hawley. The reason is that the Smoot–Hawley legislation was two years in the making and its passage was widely anticipated. Many countries with less cumbersome legislative procedures took action in advance of Smoot–Hawley's appearance on the statute book.

Some of the duties imposed led to bilateral as opposed to multilateral exchanges, and they encouraged the formation of trading blocs. Barter arrangements increased, as did clearing agreements – designed to balance exchanges between the two participating countries. There had been no agreements of that kind in 1929. By 1937 almost an eighth of the world's trade came within the scope of such agreements.

International trade

Following the First World War there were various forces disturbing international trade. Debt and reparation payments, central European hyperinflation, wartime import substitution, and so on, all played a part. In many countries demand was depressed and yet great advances in technology had resulted in hugely expanded agricultural and primary produce output. Combined with the post-war glut of shipping, this led to tumbling prices for these products. However, by the time of the re-establishment of the gold standard many of the problems appeared to be diminishing somewhat, and trade began to grow steadily.

World trade was on a greatly upward trend from the middle of the 1920s until the peak in activity in 1929. Taking 1929 as the base year for 100, world trade had grown from 94·3 in 1925, that is, by over 6 per cent in four years – steady, given the generally fragile state of the world economy. The next few years, though, saw the most dramatic destruction of trade in the history of the world economy, By 1932 the index had fallen to 39·1 – a fall of over 60 per cent in the real value of world trade in just three years. It continued to fall for the next two years, reaching a nadir of 34·0 in 1934. There was some improvement in the next few years, so that the index stood at 40·5 in 1938. But that means that world trade in 1938 was still 60 per cent below the point it had reached in 1929.

Not all the blame for this collapse should be laid at the door of the Smoot–Hawley trade wars. The US depression of 1929–33 was the deepest ever, and the fall in income was undoubtedly responsible for much of the fall in world trade. Thereafter – that is, after the initial fall in income in all countries – from 1929 onwards the two elements were inextricably bound up in driving trade and income down further. The tariffs imposed, by raising prices, reduced the demand for goods and so reduced the income earned by the exporters of goods. That in turn depressed their demand for other countries' products, and so the downward spiral went on.

It is difficult to disentangle the relative contribution of each element, but some indication can be gained from the following. At the end of the 1930s most countries had surpassed by some distance the level of GDP they had reached in 1929. World output was approximately 20 per cent higher in 1938 than the 1929 figure. And yet, as we have seen, trade was 60 per cent lower. Thus trade, which is usually closely tied to income, was drastically impaired. The loss of income which resulted from trade restrictions must be judged to have been substantial. There is also the further point that protection leads to misallocation of resources and so depresses economic welfare further.

Origins of protection

The United States

The introduction of the Smoot–Hawley tariff in 1930 is a landmark in protectionist history. The earliest explanation offered for its introduction was couched in terms of satisfying the needs of agriculture. Agriculture in many forms and all round the world had suffered throughout the 1920s. In the United States industry was booming but agriculture was depressed in the face of 'New World' expansion of agriculture and the decline in demand in Europe. There was undoubtedly something in the view that the tariff was a form of agricultural relief, but as it stood that argument failed to account for the fact that the tariff was extended to manufacturers and was supported by a number of industrial regions.

In the early years following its introduction it was portrayed as a classic case of the success of interest group lobbying (Schattschneider, 1935). The whole process of the legislation was seen as evidence of log-rolling on a grand scale. There was a long record of this kind of behaviour in the United States, but it had become increasingly refined as business cultivated government from the early twentieth century onwards, and was stimulated further by close wartime connections. Labour too was well organised, and even agriculture managed to find effective means of presenting a coherent case to government.

More recently the adoption of the tariff has been portrayed as simply an unsurprising outcome of party politics (Pastor, 1980). With the Republicans long associated with the argument in favour of protection, especially for industry, and at the same time the Democrats in the 1920s strongly opposed to protection, Pastor argues, there is no mystery about its introduction.

Eichengreen (1989) puts forward a more persuasive argument in his extension of the Gerschenkron model of interest group behaviour. He distinguishes between sheltered and unsheltered agriculture on the one hand and between light and heavy industry on the other. There were clear differences within agriculture and even between some products. Wheat, for example, was not a homogeneous product. It was the farmers close to the Canadian border who favoured protection rather than those in the Middle West or the south.

Similarly there were considerable differences in manufacturing. In this case it was light industry, concentrating on the batch production of goods tailored to a market, that was pressing most vigorously for protection. Small-scale labour-intensive firms were suffering from growing foreign competition. The net result was that border farmers sought protection but found it difficult to achieve on their own. Light industries of the kind described also favoured it but required an ally. The outcome was an alliance of the two that was successful in achieving their objectives.

British protectionism

Since the British adoption of protection was one of the most dramatic reversals of policy it deserves some extended treatment. The return to protectionist trade policies in Britain after almost a century of commitment to free trade as a genuinely serious source of concern to the world economy in the middle of the Great Depression. What led to the adoption of a policy that had had no place in British economic life for so long? The question has long been debated, and a variety of answers have been put forward. These answers chiefly take the following forms. It was a desperate measure in the face of one of the worst economic recessions in economic history. Some find that too strong, and suggest that the forces working for protection had been gaining strength in the 1920s – indeed, from as early as the First World War (McGuire, 1951; Capie, 1983). According to this latter account the return to protection was likely even without the depression of 1929–32. The third explanation emphasises the longer term. It draws on the fact that there are always groups who benefit from protection and where they can acquire power they are likely to encourage protectionism and adopt protectionist measures.

In this section these three strains are considered in reverse order. The weight of evidence appears to fall on the second, 'medium term', explanation. Finally, we turn to a brief consideration of the shape of the tariff structure that was established in Britain in the 1930s.

Britain's adoption of free trade, as noted above, came in the first half of the nineteenth century when Britain was the dominant industrial power. British textile manufacturers were enthusiastic free-traders so long as they had a virtual monopoly. That way they could delay the rise of foreign competition. Their views on free trade did not extend to machinery, since the free movement of machinery would weaken their monopoly position. For roughly a quarter of a century from the repeal of the corn laws in 1846 free trade reigned supreme in Britain.

As the nineteenth century progressed and British dominance was encroached upon more and more, the sound of free-traders began to wane and the jingle of protectionists could be heard more frequently. Just as theory predicts, there were increasingly cries from those who were suffering from competition and a number of organised attempts were made at reversing free-trade policy.

It is difficult to prove that a build-up of pressure was leading inexorably to the adoption of protection, but there is considerable suggestive evidence. After the mid-nineteenth century those who were opposed to free trade became more vocal. The Fiscal Reform League was founded in 1870 for the purpose of lobbying for the adoption of moderate duties on foreign manufactures. There was much discussion and much support from some chambers of commerce. The National Fair Trade League was formed in 1881 by just some suffering manufacturers. The tariff reform movement that grew up in these years worked diligently on all fronts and was closely associated with the movements for protection and imperial preference both at home and in empire countries. Joseph Chamberlain gave the tariff reformers fresh encouragement in the 1890s when he became Colonial Secretary and later led the tariff reform movement. However, none of these activities bore any fruit. The 1906 general election was contested with the issues of protection and imperial preference clearly in the forefront but the electorate were not persuaded. So at the outbreak of the First World War Britain remained firmly attached to the free-trade doctrine, having come through years of increasing international competition, some industrial recession and growing protectionist pressure without really wavering on the policy.

Some historians of the tariff have suggested that the implementation of protectionist legislation in 1931–32 should be seen as the culmination of a movement that was gaining strength from at least the 1923 election, an election that was fought on the issue of protection (McGuire, 1951). It takes little effort to push that date back to the First World War. War has often been a spur to protection and it is not difficult to see why. The foreigner is at his most vulnerable and the forces of protection are therefore at their most relatively powerful. Protectionist duties were introduced in wartime – the McKenna duties of 1915. But, more importantly, a committee was set up during the war to consider post-war commercial policy with a committed protectionist as its chairman. The committee strongly advocated a tariff, particularly for 'pivotal' industries. This opened the way for the Safeguarding of Industries Act to be passed in 1921, which allowed a long list of items to be given protection even if the value of goods affected was quite low. It was a victory for protection. British industries became increasingly protectionist in outlook.

In 1923 the Conservatives were seeking re-election, and the election of that year can be said to have been contested very largely on the issue of protection. There was some backing from sectors of British industry. For example, part of the textile trade had sought an order under the Safeguarding Act a matter of weeks before the election, and the iron and steel industry was working diligently for a tariff. The motor industry actively supported the protectionist case and did everything it could to persuade its workers to vote Conservative. The National Union of Manufacturers campaigned vigorously to win the working classes over (Snyder, 1944).

All this came immediately after one of the worst economic recessions in British history, 1920–21. But the electorate rejected protection and elected the first-ever Labour government. The Conservatives regained power a year later and thereafter the iron and steel industry persistently sought protection throughout the rest of the 1920s. In June 1925 an application was made to the President of the Board of Trade for duties (under the Safeguarding Act) on pig iron, wrought iron, heavy steel products and wire. Rejecting the application at the end of the year, the Prime Minister, Stanley Baldwin, said that safeguarding a basic industry of such size would have repercussions that might be held to be in conflict with the government's declaration in regard to a general tariff. Most of the executive committee of the National Federation of Iron and Steel Manufacturers and the director, Sir William Larke, were enthusiastic tariff reformers, and in early 1926 they gave their support to a sub-section of the industry, wire, when it made an independent application. But the application was rejected on the same grounds. The main application was renewed in 1927, but again it was turned down by reference to the original decision.

The Iron and Steel Confederation tried a slightly different approach the following year (1928) by asking the government to set up a committee to investigate competition in the home market. The request was refused by Baldwin, although he did say that if the Conservatives were returned at the general election of 1929 the iron and steel industry could make out a case under the safeguarding provisions. This was a shift from the government's earlier position and, together with the increasing openness of the Conservatives over protection, led the industry to be hopeful for the immediate future.

The iron and steel industry argued that protection would allow it full capacity utilisation and economies of scale such as to allow lower prices. But much of British industry remained understandably sceptical of this argument, and feared that the price of their inputs would in fact rise.

Parliament had become increasingly influenced by businessmen (as opposed to landowners or the professions), from Bonar Law the ironmaker, through Baldwin the steelmaker to the Chamberlains, who were screw manufacturers. According to one account, between 1919 and 1939 on average a third of the Conservative Party in the Commons were employers or managers (Rolf, 1974). It would be dangerous to draw conclusions too readily from a simple count of heads, bearing in mind the diversity of motives that take people into Parliament, and that numbers alone do not accurately reflect the strength of respective groupings. But clearly, the larger the numbers were, the greater was the chance that business interests were represented and the higher the probability that business demands would be heard, that numbers could be found for their support, and so on. Business groups had been accustomed to organising to achieve specific objectives for a long time and had a focus in the chambers of commerce. From the late nineteenth century an increasing number of manufacturers began to support the Conservative Party with the avowed intention of securing tariffs.

Several business organisations had been formed in the First World War with a view to defending business interests. Many of them were direct descendants of the pre-war tariff movements, but others were the product of new concerns raised by war. In January 1915, soon after the outbreak of hostilities, a Unionist Business Committee was formed in the House of Commons to protect the interest of business in time of war. A high point of business pressure for protection came with the publication of a tariff scheme adopted by the London Chamber of Commerce on 25 May 1916. The Federation of British Industries (FBI) formed in 1916, was protectionist in outlook. In 1916 the British Commonwealth Union was established 'to form a solid business group in Parliament'; a fundamental element of its programme was tariff reform, and it was linked with empire interests.

In wartime, then, the foundations were laid and in the deep recession of 1921 the Conservatives exploited the collapse in trade for their protectionist ends. A powerful deputation from the National Union of Manufacturers (NUM) visited Baldwin, then President of the Board of Trade, urging prompt action. Baldwin agreed. The Safeguarding of Industries Bill soon followed, being introduced on 2 June 1921. It met with no difficulty in its passage through Parliament and became law on 1 October. It was a clear case of the result of pressure.

A powerful pressure group evolved in the second half of the 1920s. It was the Empire Industries Association, founded in 1924. It urged apparent concern for empire with the need to protect against foreigners, and was thus ideally equipped for the particular problem of the time. It was to play an important part in advancing the protectionist case, and according to some views it gave that case the decisive thrust.

There are those who view the resort to protection as a crisis measure brought about by the need to respond to the deep economic recession. As noted, Lindert is an example. We have noted earlier that in Britain the recession was not in fact deep. However, what was striking in 1930 and 1931 was the great rise in unemployment. Unemployment is sometimes, erroneously, used as a measure of economic activity. Its use is erroneous because while it may on occasions proxy output it certainly does not always do so, and it can be affected by a number of other factors. Some of these other factors have been examined for this period and have been shown to contribute a good deal by way of explanation. The most obvious are real wages and the benefit system (Beenstock *et al.*, 1984).

Erroneous or not as a measure of depression, unemployment was still a reality that politicians had to respond to. A favourite response has always been that the blame must lie with foreigners, and demands for protection have arisen in these circumstances. This was the kind of mood that was being exploited by some in 1931.

A National Government, but one dominated by the protectionist Conservatives, came to power in the autumn of 1931 and immediately found an excuse for introducing very high tariffs. It claimed that imports in October that year were on such a scale as to constitute dumping, and something must be done about them. In fact the evidence was slender, to say the least. The government compared manufactured imports coming into the ports of London and Harwich in October 1931 and the first few days of November with those of the corresponding period in 1930. There was not much difference for October, but the early part of November did show an increase. On the strength of this the Abnormal Importation (Customs Duties) Bill was introduced in Parliament on 16 November and became law on 25 November. Duties of 100 per cent were permitted, since the Act was designed not to tax but to prevent goods coming in.

Several points should be made about this legislation. The first is that there was no good evidence of dumping. There are difficulties in defining and observing dumping. Long-term dumping below the cost of production was unlikely, given the risks. Short-term dumping, either of a sporadic or of a predatory type, was always possible and it was this latter that was feared in late 1931. The second point is that, while there was a rise in imports of some items at a time when world trade was collapsing, the likelihood is that the explanation lies in importers acting to beat the widely rumoured imposition of a tariff. Furthermore, there was a depreciation of sterling in the months following the severing of the link with gold. A third point was that the pattern of imports was often similar between products where one was expected to be protected and the other was not.

The supposed abnormal imports did not exist. The operation was simply an excuse to dramatise the government's concern and pave the way for the introduction of the general tariff which came before Parliament in February 1932 and was implemented in April the same year.

The British return to protection after almost eighty years can therefore be seen as a triumph for the business pressure that had its origins in the years before 1914 and whose real foundations are found in the First World War. Thereafter the pressure built up steadily throughout the 1920s. The performance of the economy between 1929 and 1932 was not the real cause. Unemployment was exploited, and spurious dumping was concocted to pave the way for the protectionist measures the Conservatives had long favoured.

Chapter 7

The inter-war impact

The whole international economy was in a state of considerable flux following the First World War. Industry had been severely disrupted and demand and supply patterns seriously distorted. Attempts at temporary import substitution were sometimes sufficiently successful to become permanent. Exchange rates were also out of alignment following differential price experience in the years 1914–20. In addition there were problems of war debt and reparations. New nation states were born in the aftermath of the war and more protectionism and nationalism accompanied them. All these factors meant that trading patterns were greatly changed. Further, since there were great technological advances during the war years, it is not reasonable simply to look at pre-war patterns and draw comparisons based on them, for the post-war world. Products had changed and comparative advantage had shifted.

Many of these problems led directly or indirectly to the Great Depression that afflicted so many countries in the years 1929–33. And all this makes it that much more difficult to capture the effects of the tariff. For example, the basic question – how much were imports reduced as a result of a tariff? – requires a knowledge of price elasticities. But on what data could these reasonably be estimated, given what has been said?

In this chapter we examine the results of several different approaches to analysing the effects of the tariff. Looking at effective protection proves particularly useful for this episode. The conclusion that can be drawn from the various assessments is that the tariff did not contribute significantly to the performance of the British economy in the 1930s.

Assessing the impact of any protectionist device on the whole economy is hazardous. Doing so for the Smoot–Hawley Act in the United States in the early 1930s is probably more difficult than most. It was introduced in 1930 in the early stages of what became the Great Depression. The question is, what part did it play in the Great Depression? For some, such as Kindleberger (1973), it reflected the lack of leadership that was at base the cause of the major difficulties in the world economy in the years between the two World Wars.

In a specific assessment Meltzer (1976) argued that in the absence of the tariff US prices would have fallen relative to those abroad and so increased the demand for US exports. But the tariff prevented this and so, Meltzer argues, it turned recession into deep depression. Meltzer further argued that the tariff drew gold to the United States and so led to contraction abroad, which in turn reduced the demand for American goods. This could have more then offset any increase in domestic demand. There was then the further likelihood that these features could have been exacerbated by the effects of retaliation.

Gordon and Wilcox (1981) support and advance the view of Meltzer. They see the tariff as being contractionary within the United States; foreign retaliation reduced the demand for US exports, and that situation in turn was aggravated by the Keynesian multiplier. Further, foreign retaliation in agricultural goods worsened the decline in farm prices, which contributed to rural bank failures, and the resulting decline in money supply brought about a contraction in the real economy.

The contraction came about since, according to the quantity equation, the tariff raised prices higher than they would otherwise have been. With the money stock and velocity constant, the volume of production must have fallen. Gordon and Wilcox's argument holds under floating exchange rates, and they argue that flexible rates are the appropriate framework, since the Federal Reserve sterilised gold flows over this period.

Eichengreen disputes all this, arguing instead:

> (i) that the direct effects of Smoot–Hawley were favourable for the US economy and unfavourable abroad, (ii) that the impact of the tariff on foreign demand for US exports did not offset these favourable effects, and (iii) that it is even unclear that foreign retaliation swamped these effects. [1989, p. 19]

Eichengreen's reasoning is that 'under fixed exchange rates, a tariff is expansionary for reasons related both to aggregate demand and aggregate supply . . .' (p. 20).

One of the commonest assertions is that the Smoot-Hawley tariff did greatest harm by provoking retaliation around the world. We have already noted that the retaliation was widespread. And further that, since retaliation destroyed the international monetary system – the gold standard that broke down in the 1930s – the impact came via that route. But Eichengreen argues that direct retaliation was less than is usually claimed and that Smoot–Hawley can be seen as no more than one of the forces contributing to the collapse of the international trading system. This is fine judgement over what constitutes retaliation.

Eichengreen concludes on the impact that:

> it remains likely that the tariff was expansionary even when one admits the existence of feedbacks. Further this remains possible and even plausible when the effects of foreign retaliation are introduced ... If Smoot–Hawley had significant economic effects, these operated instead through its impact on the stability of the international monetary system and the efficiency of the world's capital markets. [1989, pp. 75, 76]

In the 1930s the British economy grew faster than at any time in the previous half-century. The accepted way to measure growth is from one peak in the cycle to the next (or from one trough to the next trough), in this case from the peak in 1929 to that in 1937. Over that period the economy grew at more than 2 per cent per annum. That was faster than in the 1920s (1924–29), which in turn were better than anything since the 1870s. The depression of 1929–32 was not severe in Britain, not as deep as that of 1920–21, and mild compared with most other countries. That partly accounts for the good performance over the whole cycle. But more important was the very strong upswing of 1932–37, one of the strongest in British history. The economy grew by 24 per cent in that short period.

What brought about this remarkable growth? The tariff and some other protectionist measures were introduced in 1932, and many have been content to argue *post hoc ergo propter hoc*, that it was protection that was responsible. The main objection is that a whole host of other factors might equally contend for that position. This was a time when a great deal was heard about managing the economy. A number of policies were introduced and, as usual, there were some exogenous factors that also operated. Where the whole explanation lies is not easy to determine, and this is not the place to pursue it. Our purpose here is to consider the part the tariff may have played.

Some early assessments of the tariff, which relied on rather casual investigations, found favourably. Some attributed the fall in imports directly to the tariff. Khan (1946) claimed that imports of manufactures were reduced by 60 per cent inside eighteen months. Arthur Lewis (1949) felt that the tariff was too low to have been of much use. Benham, one of the most distinguished contemporary investigators, believed that the tariff assisted recovery by stimulating investment in iron and steel. This is of particular interest in view of some specific results that we shall turn to shortly. Finally, in a lengthier study Richardson concluded that 'the effects of the general tariff were not very significant' (1967, p. 408).

We refer here to some different approaches to investigating the impact, using more recent developments in theory and some different data.

In an earlier chapter the concept of effective protection was introduced. It has become a useful way of looking at the impact of tariffs both within an economy and when making international comparisons. It is particularly useful for looking at the likely impact of protection on resource flows – those industries getting the greatest amount of effective protection should attract more resources than those beneath them in the list. It is important to be clear that there are many difficulties in the calculation of effective rates. There are problems relating to the assumptions and there are problems of data. However, if effective rates can be derived for a reasonable coverage of British industry and ranked in order of the effective protection given, it becomes possible to talk in general terms about the likely impact. Effective rates have been calculated for British industry for this period (Capie 1978) and they allow something to be said about the likely impact of the tariff and its contribution to economic growth.

The effective rates of protection range in the main between 40 per cent and 60 per cent, and that is not surprising, since they are typically of the order of twice the size of the nominal tariff. But although that is the range there are some that lie well outside it, and they are of particular interest because of the nature of the industries involved.

One case that is of considerable interest is the construction sector. It was the biggest sector of all, almost twice the size of the next largest, iron and steel manufacturing. Much of the credit for the beginning of recovery in the early 1930s has been given to construction, particularly residential building. (A huge proportion of inter-war semi-detached houses date from 1932, as does a great deal of commercial property.) For example, Benham, writing some years after the depression, and later Richardson in one of the most thorough historical studies, have credited the building industry with the crucial contribution to the recovery. Few historians of the period since have disputed this judgement.

The great expansion in building rested on a large number of factors on both the demand and the supply side. There were demographic factors that meant a growing population of house-buying age, and this was coupled with rising real incomes for the great bulk of the population. Real wages had in fact risen quite steeply through the depression years, since money wages were relatively sticky but prices had fallen quite sharply. Supporting the demand side was an important institutional factor, and that was the availability of finance from the building societies at relatively modest interest rates. Mortgage finance was a growing area in the inter-war years and building societies prospered enormously. Thus there is no difficulty in accepting that the size of construction was such as to make whatever happened there important. There will always be questions about the precise timing, but the evidence is persuasive that this sector gave the initial boost to recovery, and thereafter contributed greatly to the strong upswing in the rest of the decade.

Having said all that, what is of interest is that the effective rate of protection for this sector was negative. This is not a controversial result. It comes about because the final product is not tradable but many of the inputs into building were tradable. So the final production, housing, had no tariff on it but importable inputs which made up 42 per cent of the final product had tariffs on them – slates, glass, timber, metal door and window frames and even bricks – at rates that ranged from 15 per cent to 33·3 per cent.

The building industry was therefore taxed more heavily than, was put at a disadvantage in relation to, the rest of industry. Even if refinements are added to the effective protection result, there is little prospect of the construction sector coming off the bottom of the list. In other words, resources will have been pulled away from this sector and attracted to others. The point to stress is that, even acknowledging that the industry contributed greatly to economic recovery, it has to be accepted that the tariff diminished its contribution.

A similar point has to be made about the iron and steel industry. It comes out next to bottom in the rankings of effective protection. This industry, again partly by virtue of its size, is one that reputedly gave great stimulus to recovery. The nature of the industry makes the calculation of the effective rate more difficult than in many other cases. The industry consisted of two main parts. There was what was called the 'heavy' part that produced pig iron, semi-finished products and the simpler rolled products. And there was the 'light' part, where re-rolling and finishing were carried out along with the production of more specialised goods. The raw material passes through so many stages before it reaches its final form that it is difficult to define the industry. Some firms covered most processes.

It was mostly those firms engaged in the 'heavy' end of the industry which actively sought the tariff and those in the 'light' end that were opposed to it. The heavy end was dominant in every way, and it was the 'heavy' firms that were successful in obtaining high tariffs. The light end resisted the tariff of 33·3 per cent on its raw materials and semi-finished products, even though it was given a 20 per cent tariff on the finished product. It was one of those rare occasions in tariff history when the tariff imposed on the input was greater than that on the final product. The end result was an effective rate of protection that was very low.

Here, then, is an industry which was given little protection – least by far of all in the manufacturing sector – and yet this industry is credited with having made the greatest contribution of all manufacturing industries to the recovery. Accepting that it did make such a contribution, we are nevertheless forced to conclude that it was handicapped by the tariff. We would have to look elsewhere for the reasons – possibly to the rationalisation of the industry. The tariff would have resulted in resources being drawn away from iron and steel.

These two sectors – construction and iron and steel – which come at the bottom of the rankings of effective protection made up almost 40 per cent of total industrial output. These are the two sectors that are said to have contributed most to the very strong surge in economic activity from 1932 to 1937. They were both considerably handicapped by the tariff, and on this basis we would have to conclude that the contribution of the tariff to economic revival was minimal.

Although these results on effective protection have become quite widely accepted, and have added to our understanding of the role of the tariff, they have not gone unchallenged. Some objections have been raised to the restrictive assumptions employed in the effective protection model (Foreman-Peck, 1981), and some dispute has arisen over the precise amount of inputs in some industries (Kitson *et al.*, 1991). These complaints have, however, led to some alternative explorations of the issue and yielded some interesting results.

For example, in one of these other approaches Foreman-Peck used a simple Keynesian model in order to assess the effects of the tariff on the overall level of demand. He therefore estimates the reduction in imports brought about by the tariff between the years 1930 and 1935. He found a 32·7 per cent fall in manufactured imports in a period when income rose by 6 per cent. Having estimated a propensity to import manufactured and semi-manufactured goods of 1·44, Foreman-Peck employs that figure to show that income should have raised imports by 8·6 per cent. Therefore protection was actually responsible for a fall in imports of almost 41 per cent, the income rise bringing it back to an actual level of 32·7.

There would therefore have been a switch to domestic goods as a result of the tariff. And, added to that, some multiplier should be used to estimate and indicate the overall contribution of the tariff. Foreman-Peck uses Kahn's multiplier estimate of 1·75. This leads to the conclusion that 2·3 percentage points of the total rise of 24 per cent can be attributed to the tariff.

There are several problems with the approach, not the least of which is the attribution of the fall in imports to the tariff. Although the British economy was not in serious recession, a large part of the rest of the world industrial economy was; world trade had collapsed dramatically between 1929 and 1932 and had slipped further by 1935. British imports fell from a value of £1,044 million in 1930 to £861 million (17·5 per cent) *before* the tariff was imposed. Income fell by 5·6 per cent that year, which on these figures should have brought about an (approximately) 8 per cent fall in imports. Something else must account for the bulk of the fall. Imports fell by a further 18·5 per cent to £702 million in 1932, when for most of that year tariffs were at their initial level of 10 per cent. The following year there was another fall, but some of it must be attributed to the exchange rate. Thus, even without the tariff, imports were falling. We must look elsewhere for the explanation and should not attribute the fall in imports exclusively to the tariff. We must therefore modify any expenditure switching calculation and income-generating effects that are said to be attributable to the tariff.

Britain had returned to the gold standard in 1925 and remained on it until 1931. The debate on protection had taken place in the context of a fixed exchange rate regime. International trade theory deals with the differential impacts that can be expected from tariffs under fixed and floating exchange rates regimes. The basic position is that the tariff can be effective under fixed rates, though, as was noted above, the extent will be affected by the impact on the money supply and the general price level changes (Brunner, 1976). But tariffs will be ineffective and possibly perverse under floating rates.

Britain left the gold standard in September 1931 and shortly thereafter implemented protectionist policies. It was at this stage that Keynes gave up his advocacy of the tariff. On leaving the gold standard Britain did not, however, permit the pound to float completely freely. It was at this time that the Exchange

Equalisation Account was established and the exchange rate entered a period of dirty floating. Under fixed exchange rates a tariff diverts demand to home goods. Domestic output can thus be encouraged, and incomes raised. But under a floating rate there is ultimately no change. Within a simple macroeconomic framework with floating rates, the tariff would bring about a rightward shift in the IS curve and a rise in interest rates. That would induce a capital inflow and so lead to an appreciation in the exchange rate. A rise in sterling would then divert demand from home goods back to imports, and the process would continue until interest rates were back at their initial point. Hence there should be no expectation that protection should contribute to economic growth. In fact Mundell (1968) went further than this, showing that under floating rates a new tariff was likely to be contractionary – it would actually reduce national output and income.

Eichengreen (1981) has argued that the tariff was implemented not as an anti-unemployment policy but 'rather as an attempt to strengthen the trade balance and prevent the exchange rate from depreciating excessively'. Further, that there was little faith in the power of floating rates to correct the current account deficit which had appeared. Eichengreen's view is that because of the experience of several countries in the 1920s, notably that of Germany, the fear of the time was of dramatic exchange rate depreciation and consequent hyperinflation. The policy-makers, he argues, imposed the tariff in the knowledge that it might exacerbate unemployment, and this was a price to be paid for exchange rate and price stability. This line of reasoning is surely ahistorical for the British economy at that time. Even in the 1920s prices in Britain were falling. They fell more steeply in the world recession. Businessmen and policy-makers craved price rises in 1931. Anything that could be done to raise prices was done. It was deflation that they feared, and felt was damaging.

Kitson and Solomou's (1990) is the most recent attempt at estimating the impact of the tariff in Britain in the 1930s. Their main contribution has been the estimation of a model purporting to explain manufacturing imports, a means of distinguishing between different policies, but particularly those on the exchange rate and protection. There are serious difficulties with their procedure, though they conclude favourably on protection, if without much precision. The strongest statement they make is: 'An overview of the natural influences on the recovery suggests that it is the *interaction* of a changed trade policy with the 'natural' influences that explain why Britain performed well in the 1930s . . .' (p. 99).

The principal aspect that is not taken into account by these writers is the impact British protectionism had on the rest of the world. The impact on the international economy has been alluded to above. Britain was still the major trading country in the world economy, and when it took the measures it did there were all manner of responses around the world. To Isolate the domestic impact of tariffs in Britain is to ignore this aspect and its ramifications for world trade. The reverberations that undoubtedly swept around the world and back to Britain can have done only harm to British external trade and hence to British economic growth.

Chapter 8

Conclusion

Protectionist commercial policies can be found in almost every period in the history of the world economy. But there have been periods when their intensity and extent have increased, and these periods can be seen as predominantly protectionist. One such notable period was the late nineteenth century. Another was the period between the two World Wars. A third is the period we are now living through. The rise in protection over the last twenty years has been charted in the publications of the IMF and the World Bank. The questions that arise are: how concerned should we be about the current rise in protection? What will the likely outcome be? The argument of this book is that, if there are lessons in history, then there are dangers in the worldwide trend towards protectionism in international trade. The ultimate collapse of trade is the most serious danger, and the concomitant fall in income could lead to deep depression.

Consider the recent threat of tariff wars. Are there parallels to be drawn between the present day and the inter-war years? Can lessons be learned from that previous experience? History never quite repeats itself. But there certainly are comparisons that are worth making and there are surely lessons that can be learned. It is clear that there have been dangers in the world trading system for some years now. One of the lessons is that it is not sensible to assume that the politicians and/or trade negotiators could never be so foolish as to allow a catastrophe to happen. There seems always to be an assumption that the present time (whenever that time might be) mankind has reached a high point of knowledge and wisdom, and no foolish decisions will be taken. And unfortunately there is ignorance of history. One of the striking parallels from the experience of the inter-war years is that at the time there seemed to be widespread acceptance at governmental level of the desirability of free trade. Conferences were organised by the League of Nations where all the delegates would make speeches on the desirability of free trade, then invariably go home and raise protectionist barriers to satisfy powerful domestic producers or some other electorally important body.

Another lesson is that there is no safety and security in trading blocs such as the EC could become. Trade blocs are an unsatisfactory substitute for free trade. It was a dream of some in the 1930s to make the British empire self-sufficient, with Britain producing the manufactured goods and the other countries the food and raw materials. But even in the 1930s, when the world was less integrated than it is now, that could be seen as the chimera it was. There were too many links with other countries. Some empire countries had closer ties with foreign countries than they had with other empire countries. Comparative advantage does not arrange itself neatly within political boundaries. In the modern world it would be more difficult and potentially more dangerous to seek self-sufficiency in such trading blocs.

A further and important lesson is to recognise that once they start, tariff wars acquire a dangerous momentum of their own. There is no predicting their course or their end. It is easy to adopt a measure in order to assert one's position or to establish a basis for future negotiation. But it is much more difficult to control the clamour for such measures, and nearly impossible to remove them in the short term. And irrationality then takes over – with otherwise responsible 'statesmen' seriously threatening tit-for-tat.

Almost everyone accepts that, while protection may benefit some groups within the economy, free trade is the better policy for the community at large. Yet, as we have seen, in 1992 and 1993 protectionist measures have been threatened by both sides in the dispute between the United States and the European Community, ignoring the damage they would necessarily do to themselves in the process. Nor can there be any guarantee that the dispute can be limited to the initial disputants. There are no winners in trade wars. It is surely time for another determined onslaught on existing protectionist measures.

The greatest growth in world trade and development has come in periods when trading conditions were at their most liberal – in the nineteenth century and in the years after the Second World War. Economic openness, and the maximum possible exposure to the world economy through freedom of trade, lead to economic development and use existing resources in a better way.

Another outcome is possible, less serious for the world economy but nevertheless potentially ruinous for some individual countries. It may be, as in the examples given above, that protection does not seriously harm the principal industrial economies. No great damage may be done and no great aggregate benefits accrue. But some countries dependent on access to the leading economies could suffer a great deal. They will often be Third World primary producers, though not necessarily so. One obvious case is New Zealand. New Zealand is a small country that used to be prosperous, the prosperity deriving from an efficient agricultural sector. Relatively free from retaliation, New Zealand misguidedly adopted protectionist measures in the 1950s, but abandoned them in the 1980s. However, by then the economy was in serious decline as a result of the agricultural protectionism of the European Community. New Zealand lost the main outlet for its efficiently produced lamb and diary produce when Britain joined the Common Market. Such examples have proliferated in the international economy.

The policy prescription from international trade theory is virtually unambiguous and has been accepted by most economists for almost two centuries. It is that free trade is the policy that raises national and international welfare. Unilateral free trade would be accepted by the majority of economists. The reason is that the exploitation of comparative advantage allows the optimal division and specialisation of labour and hence the greatest output. But the same trade theory also shows how the gains from trade are distributed and who the gainers and losers are in different circumstances. It therefore holds the key to an understanding of why pressures for protection arise, and of why and when such pressures are likely to be successful.

Some recent developments in the theory have attempted to allow for conditions in the real world in a more realistic way than the commonly used perfectly competitive model. These new developments, admitting the coexistence of increasing returns with imperfect competition, show that there may be occasions when intervention can raise welfare. But, as has been remarked, even the exponents of these views concede that, when all other points are considered, free trade is the best policy to adhere to.

Why then, if there is such rare universal agreement among economists about a policy, in this case the desirability of free trade, has it been such a struggle to achieve it? There are some grand theories that offer explanations in terms of (for example) hegemonic power, or the collapse of an old order. But in the modern world economy the key to the explanation lies in the triumph of interest groups. That might be thought rather obvious at the present time when we see well-to-do European farmers benefiting from higher prices than a free market would yield, simply because they still have sufficient political power. It has long been the case. In 1937 Lionel Robbins wrote, 'The evils of agrarian protectionism have become so conspicuous that their existence is not open to serious question' (1937, p. 49). And yet almost sixty years later the evils have multiplied enormously and the European Community seems impotent in the face of them. There is nevertheless something of a puzzle here, for the number of farmers has been diminishing steadily over the period. There must be some willingness on the part of others to accept the 'agricultural' argument. This takes us back to Henderson's argument on the power of the 'wrong' ideas (see pp. 22–4).

The ability of interest groups to triumph has not always been sufficiently emphasised. For example, while there may have been ready acceptance of the view that it was European agrarian interests that were responsible for the rise of protection, it is not so widely recognised (or often presented) that the British adoption of free trade in the nineteenth century was also influenced by self-interest – that of Manchester textile manufacturers with a virtual monopoly. (There have always been those who argue for free trade from basic principles. *The Economist* was founded in 1844 with the express purpose of campaigning for free trade. It has never been captured by interest groups and has never deviated from its advocacy of the principle.)

In the later nineteenth century, when arable farming in particular was suffering, Britain was not subject to the damaging pressure for protection that Europe was, since by that time Britain had largely got out of agriculture. However, by the inter-war years, when Parliament was becoming dominated by business interests, business was in large part responsible for the return to protection. And we noted similar interest-group activity in the United States.

Economic depression is sometimes advanced as the reason for protection, but we have shown that that is not the case – not for Europe in the nineteenth century and not for Britain between the wars. It may on occasion be used as the excuse, or may arguably be the trigger, but it is not the fundamental cause.

We have also argued that despite assertions to the contrary the impact of protection on the countries implementing it has rarely been large, though the question of what is large and what is not is difficult. Johnson (1960) provided a rough-and-ready reckoner for calculating the size of the impact of protection. He based it on moderately high rates of protection for economies with quite high import ratios and showed that the impact almost always worked out as very small. However, this calculation did ignore the effects of protection in reducing domestic competition and incentives, as also the effect of preventing the transfer of knowledge through trade contacts.

Economists know all too little about the causes of economic growth and essentially nothing about how to generate it. The causes are manifold and inextricably bound up together. Therefore it will always be the case that when one ingredient is singled out for examination it is going to give a weak result. But that does not alter the fact that that result may nevertheless be the best that there is to go on. On the evidence available, tariffs did not improve economic performance in any significant way in the nineteenth or twentieth century.

If the impact is commonly relatively small, why they should there be concern over the rise of protectionism? The reason lies in the fact that protection does diminish trade. That, after all, is the point of it. And while it is often true that the effect of the tariff can be avoided to some extent, there is no escaping the fact that trade is impaired. As we have noted, the accompanying fall in some countries has sometimes been steep. There follow declines in shipping and services and so on. And the likelihood is that retaliation will take place, leading to further losses in trade and income. The fact that protection breeds this kind of response means that the destruction of international trade is threatened, and that makes protection such a danger. Furthermore, quantitative restrictions (used extensively in the 1930s) are the most damaging form of protection and usually imply very high implicit rates of protection. The effects on income distribution are also significant, those with political clout shifting income their way.

Cobden, the great advocate of free trade in the nineteenth century, argued his case in good part on the proposition that free trade meant more trade, and closer relations between countries, and that this would encourage peace. To the extent that the nineteenth century was a long period of relatively free trade and of relative peace, his claims have some justification. And the fact that rising protectionism culminated in war at the end of that period lends further support.

References

Ashley, W. (1910), *Modern Tariff History*, John Mullany, London.

Bailey, S. H. (1932), 'The political aspect of discrimination in international economic relations', *Eca*, 89–115.

Bairoch, P. (1972), 'Free trade and European economic development in the nineteenth century', *European Economic Review*.

Beenstock, Michael (1983), *The World Economy in Transition*, Allen & Unwin, London.

Beenstock, Michael, Capie, Forrest, and Griffiths, Brian (1984), 'Economic Recovery in the United Kingdom in the 1930s', Bank of England Academic Panel Paper 23.

Benham, F. C. C. (1941), *Great Britain under Protection*, Macmillan, New York.

Bhagwati, Jagdish (1988), *Protectionism*, MIT Press, Cambridge, Mass.

Bhagwati, Jagdish (1991), *The World Trading System at Risk*, Harvester, Brighton.

Brander, J., and Spencer (1981), 'Tariffs and the extraction of foreign monopoly rents under potential entry', *Canadian Journal of Economics*.

Brander, J. & Spencer (1984), 'Tariff protection and imperfect competition', in H. Kierzkowski (ed.), *Monopolistic Competition and International Trade*, Oxford University Press, Oxford.

Brunner, K. (1976), 'A Fisherian framework for the analysis of international monetary problems', in Michael Parkin and George Zis (eds.), *Inflation in the World Economy*, Manchester University Press, Manchester.

Burns, A., and Mitchell, W. (1946), *Measuring Business Cycles*, NBER, New York.

Capie, Forrest (1978), 'The British tariff and industrial protection in the 1930s', *Economic History Review*.

Capie, Forrest (1983a), 'Tariff protection and economic performance, in J. Black and A. Winters (eds.), *Policy and Performance in International Trade*, Macmillan, London.

Capie, Forrest (1983b), *Depression and Protectionism: Britain between the Wars*, Allen & Unwin, London.

Capie, Forrest (1991), 'Effective protection and economic recovery in Britain, 1932–37', *Economic History Review*.

Capie, Forrest, ed. (1992), *Protectionism in the World Economy*, Edward Elgar, Aldershot.

Cmnd 1938, *Reports on Tariff Wars between certain European States*.

Conybeare, John A. C. (1987), *Trade Wars: the Theory and Practice of International Commercial Rivalry*, Columbia University Press, New York.

Corden, W. M. (1971), *The Theory of Protection*, Oxford University Press, London.

Corden, W. M. (1974), *Trade Policy and Economic Welfare*, Oxford University Press, London.

Corden, W. M. (1990), 'Strategic Trade Policy: How New? How Sensible?' World Bank W.P.S. 396.

Crafts, N. F. R. (1983), 'Gross national product in Europe, 1870–1910: some new estimates', *Explorations in Economic History.*

Davis, R. (1966), The rise of protectionism in England, 1689–1786', *Economic History Review.*

Eichengreen, B. (1981), *Sterling and the Tariff*, Princeton Studies, Prentice-Hall, Englewood Cliffs, N.J.

Eichengreen, B. (1989), 'The political economy of the Smoot–Hawley tariff', *Research in Economic History.*

Eichengreen, B. (1992), 'The eternal fiscal question', in Forrest Capie (ed.), *Protectionism in the World Economy*, Edward Elgar, Aldershot.

Falkus, M. (1972), *The Industrialisation of Russia, 1700–1914*, Macmillan, London.

Findlay, R. (1987), 'Free trade and protection', in *The New Palgrave: a Dictionary of Economics*, Macmillan, London.

Foreman-Peck, J. (1981), 'The British tariff and industrial protection in the 1930s: an alternative model', *Economic History Review.*

Foreman-Peck, J. (1983), *A History of World Economy: International Economic Relations*, Wheatsheaf, Brighton.

Gallarotti, Guillio (1985), 'Towards a business cycle model of tariffs', *International Organisation.*

Gerschenkron, A. (1943), *Bread and Democracy in Germany*, Cornell University Press, Ithaca, N.Y.

Gordon, M. (1941), *Barriers to World Trade: a study of recent Commercial Policy*, Kelley, New York.

Gordon, Robert J., and Wilcox, James A. (1981), 'Monetarist interpretations of the Great Depression: an evaluation and critique', in Karl Brunner (ed), *The Great Depression*

Revisited, Kluwer, Dordrecht.

Hawke, G. E. (1975), 'The United States tariff and industrial protection in the late nineteenth century', *Economic History Review*.

Henderson, David (1986), *Innocence and Design*, Blackwell, Oxford.

Henderson, David (1991), 'The evolution of the world trading system', in John Llewllyn and Stephen J. Cotter (eds.), *Economic Policies for the 1990s*, Blackwell, Oxford.

Humphrey, D.D. (1955), *American Imports*, Twentieth Century Fund, New York.

Imlah, A. H. (1958), *Economic Elements of the Pax Britannica*, Harvard University Press, Cambridge, Mass.

Isaacs, A. (1948), *International Trade: Tariffs and Commercial Policy*, Irwin, Chicago.

Johnson, H. G. (1960), 'The cost of protection and the scientific tariff', *Journal of Political Economy*.

Kenwood, A. G. and Lougheed, A. G. (1982), *The Growth of the International Economy*, Croom Helm, London.

Khan, A. E. (1946), *Great Britain in the World Economy*, Columbia University Press, New York.

Kindleberger, Charles P. (1985), 'The rise of free trade in western Europe, 1820–75', *Journal of Economic History*.

Kindleberger, Charles P. (1973), *The World in Depression*, Longman, London.

Kirchner, Walter (1981), 'Russian tariffs and foreign industries before 1919', *Journal of Economic History*.

Kitson, M. and Solomou, S. (1990), *Protectionism and Economic Revival: the British Interwar Economy*, Cambridge University Press, Cambridge.

Kitson, M, Solomou, S., and Weale, M. (1991), 'Effective protection and economic recovery in the UK during the

1930s', *Economic History Review.*

Krugman, Paul (1987), 'Is free trade *passé*', *Journal of Economic Perspectives.*

Krugman, Paul, ed. (1986), *Strategic Trade Policy and the New International Economic Order*, MIT Press Cambridge, Mass.

Lake, David (1988), *Power, Protection and Free Trade: International Sources of US Commercial Strategy, 1887–1939*, Cornell University Press, Ithaca, N.Y.

Lewis, W. A. (1949), *Economic Survey*, Allen & Unwin, London.

Liepman, H. (1938), *Tariff Levels and the Economic Unity of Europe*, Allan & Unwin, London.

Lindert, Peter H. (1991), *International Economics*, Irwin, Homewood, Ill.

Lipsey, Robert (1963), *Price and Quantity Trends in the Foreign Trade of the United States*, Columbia University Press, New York.

Meltzer, A. H. (1976), 'Monetary and other explanations for the Great Depression', *Journal of Monetary Economics.*

McCloskey, D. (1980), 'Magnanimous Albion: free trade and Britain's national income, 1841–81', *Explorations in Economic History.*

Mitchell, B. R. (1987), *European Historical Statistics, 1750–1975*, Macmillan, London.

Mundell, R. A. (1968), *International Economics*, Macmillan, New York.

McGuire, E. B. (1951), *The British Tariff System*, Methuen, London.

Nye, John Vincent (1991), 'The myth of free-trade Britain and fortress France: tariffs and trade in the nineteenth century', *Journal of Economic History.*

Pastor, Robert, A. (1980), *Congress and the Politics of US Foreign Economic Policy, 1929–76*, University of California Press, Berkeley and Los Angeles.

Pollard, S. (1981), *Peaceful Conquest*, Oxford University Press, Oxford.

Richardson, H. W. (1967), *Economic Recovery in Britain, 1932–39*, Weidenfeld & Nicolson, London.

Robbins, L. (1937), *Economic Planning and International Order*, Macmillan, London.

Robbins, L. (1976), *Political Economy Past and Present*, Macmillan, London.

Rogowski, R. (1989), *Commerce and Coalitions: how Trade affects Domestic Political Alignments*, Princeton University Press, Princeton, N.J.

Rolf, K. W. D. (1974), 'Tories, tariffs and elections: the West Midlands in English Policies, 1918–35', Ph.D thesis, Cambridge University.

Saul, S. B. (1960), *Studies in British Overseas Trade, 1870–1914*, Liverpool University Press, Liverpool.

Saul, S. B. (1969), *The Myth of the Great Depression in England*, Macmillan, London.

Schattschneider, E. E. (1935), *Politics, Pressure and the Tariff*, Prentice-Hall, New York.

Scott, M. F. G., Corden, W. M., and Little, I. M. D. (1980), *The Case against General Import Restrictions*, Trade Policy Research Centre, London.

Snyder, R. C. (1940), 'Commerical policy as reflected in treaties from 1931–39', *American Economic Review*.

Snyder, R. K. (1944), *The Tariff Problem in Great Britain, 1918–23*, Stanford University Press, Stanford, Cal.

Sombart, W. (1929), 'Economic theory and economic history', *Economic History Review*.

Sundararajan, V. (1970), 'The impact of the tariff on some selected products of the US iron and steel industry', *Quarterly Journal of Economics.*

Taussig, F. W. (1921), *Principles of Economics*, Macmillan, New York.

Toniolo, G. (1977), 'Effective protection and industrial growth: the case of Italian engineering, 1898–1913', *Journal of European Economic History.*

Webb, S. B. (1977), 'Tariff protection from the iron industry, cotton textiles and agriculture in Germany, 1879–1914', *Jahrubücher für Nationalökonomie und Statistik*, 183.

Webb, S. B. (1981), 'Tariffs, cartels, technology and growth in the German steel industry, 1879–1914', *Journal of Economic History.*

Whitney, W. (1973), 'The Structure of the American Economy in the late Nineteenth Century', University of Pennsylvania Discussion Papers 80.

Index

Der Autor

Schauspieler und leidenschaftlicher Koch Udo Thies entdeckte seine Liebe zum Ruhrgebiet während seiner Ausbildung an der Westfälischen Schauspielschule in Bochum. Er spielt regelmäßig an den Theatern Essen, Oberhausen und Bochum und hat lange im Ruhrgebiet gelebt. Seine Liebe zur Kulinarik wurde schon früh geprägt – Vater Weinhändler, Mutter begeisterte Hobbyköchin, die Großeltern hatten eine Gastwirtschaft. Und schließlich gibt es auf der Bühne und am Herd zahlreiche Parallelen: Um die Gäste zu überzeugen, braucht es Liebe, Leidenschaft und zahlreiche Proben.

Markus Krebs hat er zum ersten Mal bei einer Comedy-Nacht in Köln vor etwa Zehntausend Menschen erlebt und war tief beeindruckt. Da sitzt einer alleine mit Wollmütze und Sonnenbrille auf einem Barhocker und erzählt einen Witz nach dem anderen. So ein Ruhrpott-Typ eben, der in der Eckkneipe mit 'nem Pils neben einem sitzen könnte. Pointen, Gags und Witze sind die Königsdisziplin auf der Bühne. Hut ab und Verneigung!

Vielen Dank

FÜR DIE UNTERSTÜTZUNG BEI DER REALISIERUNG DIESES BUCHES

Löwensenf König Pilsener DON PAPA RUM Asbach Uralt

Ende Gelände

ZUM
HOCKER
Ruhrpott

ZUM HOCKER

KöPi-Sekt-Bowle mit Zitrone
Oppas Mischung

PILSKEN GEHT JA IMMER

REZEPTUR FÜR 6 BOWLER:

2 Flaschen	Weißwein
3	Bio-Zitronen
150 g	Zucker
2 Flaschen	König Pilsener
2 Flaschen	Sekt

MACH MA':

Zitrone heiß abwaschen, dann in dünne Scheiben schneiden und in das Bowle-Glas geben.

Die Hälfte des Zuckers ins Bowle-Glas geben, dann König Pilsener und Sekt einfüllen. Abschmecken! Erst dann nach Geschmack den restlichen Zucker zugeben – oder auch nicht.

Sehr erfrischend in heißen Sommernächten!

Gin-Cocktail Negroni

HERB, BITTER, FRUCHTIG, EIN APERITIF, WIE ER IM BUCHE STEHT. EIN ALLESKÖNNER. VORBEREITER, BEGLEITER UND AM ENDE KOMMT ER – ÄHNLICH WIE BEIM FUßBALL – ZUM ABSCHLUSS. VOLLTREFFER!

ZUTATEN PRO GLAS:

3 cl	Gin
3 cl	roter Wermut
3 cl	Campari
1	Orangenzeste
1	Rosmarin

HAU WECH:

Einen niedrigen Tumbler mit Eis füllen, um das Glas zu kühlen.

Zunächst den Gin einfüllen, dann Campari und Wermut, anschließend verrühren. Mit Rosmarin und Orangenzeste garnieren und ggf. mit Eis auffüllen.

> „STEHKNEIPEN SIND SO BELIEBT, WEIL DER ALKOHOL HIER DAS BESTE GEFÄLLE HAT."
>
> – JÜRGEN VON MANGER –

„Ich trinke kein Wasser, wegen der ekelhaften Sachen, welche Fische darin tun."

W. C. Fields – Amerikanischer Komiker

BEGLEITENDE GETRÄNKE

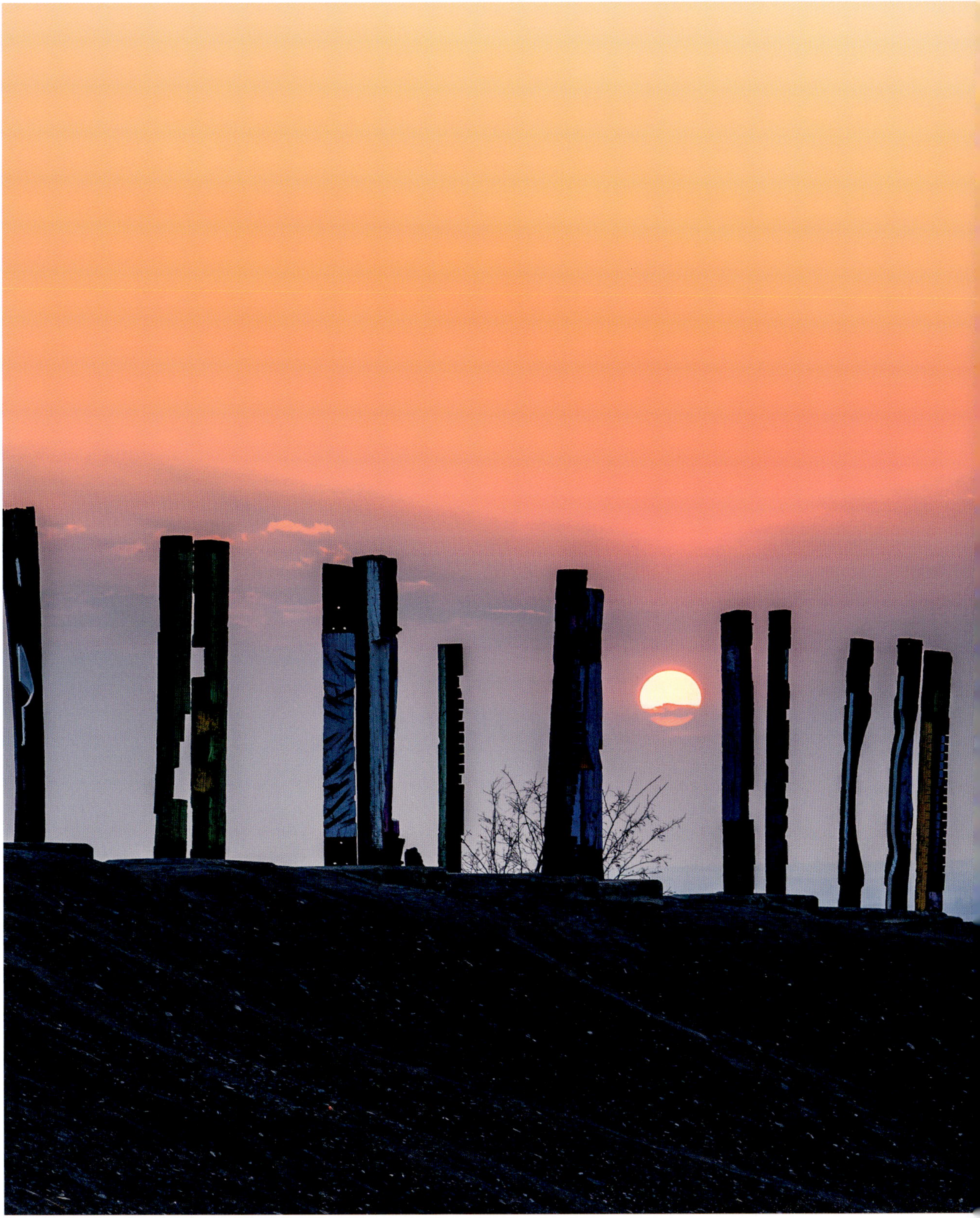

Apfelpfannküchlein MUTTER KREBS

OPPA HAT DIE ÄPFEL GEPFLÜCKT UND OMMA HAT GEZAUBERT ... MÜSSEN WARM UND FRISCH WECH, SONST - OBACHT - VOM BIERDECKEL SCHWER ZU UNTERSCHEIDEN ... MERKSTE DANN ABER BEIM KAUN ... WENNE NIX MERKST, MUSSE HEIM ...

ZUTATEN FÜR 8 STÜCK:

2	Äpfel
1 Glas	Asbach Uralt
70 g	Mehl
1 Msp.	Backpulver
1 Prise	Salz
175 ml	Milch
1	Ei
1 EL	flüssige Butter
1 EL	Vanillezucker
	Zucker/Zimt
	Butter oder Öl zum Braten

SO GEHT'S:

Äpfel schälen, entkernen und in dünne Ringe schneiden. Einige Zeit in Asbach Uralt ziehen lassen.

Milch, Butter und Eigelb verrühren. Mehl, Backpulver und Salz mischen und die Ei-Mischung unterrühren. Eiweiß mit Vanillezucker steif schlagen und unter den Teig heben.

Butter/Öl erhitzen und Pfannkuchenteig in Portionen in die Pfanne geben. Einige Apfelringe auflegen und die Pfannkuchen von beiden Seiten leicht bräunen lassen. Zucker und Zimt drüberstreuen und servieren.

Eierkuchen Hohensyburg mit beschwipsten Trockenpflaumen

SCHICKOBELLO! SIMPEL, ABER HOLLA, DIE WALDFEE!

ZUTATEN:

200 g	Trockenpflaumen
150 ml	Don Papa Rum
180 g	Mehl
½ l	Milch
125 ml	Sahne
80 g	Zucker
	gesalzene Butter
5	Eier

SO GEHT'S:

Nachdem die Trockenpflaumen einige Stunden lässig in Don Papa Rum herumgelegen haben, die Feuerstelle auf 180 °C (Ober-/Unterhitze) vorheizen.

Milch erhitzen und die Sahne hinzugeben. Mehl, Eier und Zucker vermischen und unterrühren bis ein glatter Teig entstanden ist. Eine Springform mit Butter einfetten, den Teig hineingeben und die Pflaumen darauf verteilt einsinken lassen.

45 Minuten backen, dann aus dem Ofen holen, der jubelnden Menge zeigen und den Applaus demütig entgegennehmen. Vorhang!

WENN 'NE SCHRAUBE LOCKER IST, HAT DAS LEBEN ETWAS SPIEL.

Rote-Beete-Schokotaler

Schalker Kreisel

ICH MEINE, REIN OPTISCH EIN STATEMENT ZUM RUHRGEBIET. VOM EIERBRIKETT NUR AM GESCHMACK ZU UNTERSCHEIDEN. BITTE PROBIEREN – NICHT DIE BRIKETTS, DIE SCHOKOTALER!

ZUTATEN FÜR 12 SCHOKOS:

2	Rote Beeten, vorgegart
120 g	Mandelmehl
100 g	Zartbitterschokolade
2 EL	Kokosöl
50 g	Zucker
30 g	Butter

WIE'S GEMACHT WIRD:

Den Backofen auf 180 °C (Umluft) vorheizen, eine Muffinform mit Butter einfetten. Die Schokolade klein hacken, die Rote Beete erst in kleine Stücke schneiden, dann pürieren.

In einer Schüssel Zucker, Kokosöl, Mandelmehl, Rote-Beete-Püree verrühren und am Schluss die gehackte Schokolade unterheben.

Die Masse in die Muffinform geben und 25 Minuten backen. Raus mit den Schokotalern und abkühlen lassen. Ein großartiger Duft verbreitet sich im ganzen Haus. Könnte sein, dass jetzt Nachbarn klingeln und dann müsst ihr entscheiden …

Münsterländer Stippmilch

SCHICHT IM SCHACHT

SOZUSAGEN SCHWARZWÄLDER KIRSCHTORTE IM GLAS. GIB MIR DIE KIRSCHE!, WIE MAN BEIM FUßBALL SAGT. ES WIRD AUCH VON ASBACH URALT GEMUNKELT, DER DEN PUMPERNICKEL GEFÜGIG MACHEN SOLL ... NA JA ... DER WESTFALE ... SO ISSER ...!

ZUTATEN FÜR 4:

100 g	Pumpernickel
200 g	Magerquark
200 g	Frischkäse
2 EL	Asbach Uralt
2 EL	Milch
½	Bio-Zitrone, Abrieb
1 TL	Zucker

FÜR DAS KIRSCHKOMPOTT:

100 g	Kirschen
1 TL	Vanillezucker
100 g	Kirschgelee

AUFGEPASST:

Pumpernickel klein krümeln oder schneiden und 15 Minuten in Asbach Uralt einweichen. Bio-Zitrone waschen und die Schale abreiben. In einer Schüssel Quark und Frischkäse mit Zitronenabrieb, Zucker, Vanillezucker und Milch cremig rühren.

Für das Kirschkompott alle Zutaten verrühren.

Jetzt wird geschichtet: 1 EL Quarkmasse in Gläser füllen, darauf das Kirschkompott und betrunkene Pumpernickelwürfel verteilen. Das Ganze noch einmal wiederholen.

Die Stippmilchgläser 30 Minuten im Kühlschrank durchkühlen lassen. Danach servieren und dankbar die Lobhudeleien entgegennehmen ...

Zebraküchlein Nordkurve

FANARTIKEL MSV DUISBURG ...

ZUTATEN FÜR 12 ZEBRAS:

180 g	Mehl
60 g	Zucker
60 g	weiche Butter
1 TL	Backpulver
100 ml	Milch
2 EL	Kakaopulver
1 Schuss	Don Papa Rum

OBACHT:

Backofen auf 180 °C (Ober-/Unterhitze) vorheizen und eine Muffinform bereitlegen.

Butter, Zucker, Vanilleextrakt und Salz cremig schlagen. Die Eier einrühren. Mehl und Backpulver mischen und in den Teig einarbeiten. Anschließend die Milch dazu.

Nun wird der Teig in zwei Hälften geteilt. Eine Hälfte kriegt einen Schuss Don Papa Rum und die andere Backkakao.

Jetzt werden Zebras gemacht: Form füllen mit 1–2 TL vom hellen Teig, dann 1–2 TL vom dunklen Teig mutig und mittig draufgeben. So weitermachen bis beide Teige aufgebraucht sind.

Die Form in den Backofen und 20 Minuten backen. Raus damit und runterkommen bzw. auskühlen lassen.

Dicker Reis mit Rumpflaumen

BRIKETTS IM NEUSCHNEE

KINDHEITSERINNERUNGEN WERDEN WACH, REIS MIT ZUCKER UND ZIMT ODER EBEN MIT FRÜCHTEN KENNT MAN UND LIEBT MAN VIELLEICHT NOCH HEUTE. ABER WEHE, DIE ERINNERUNG STELLT SICH NICHT EIN UND ES SCHMECKT EINFACH NICHT WIE FRÜHER!
ALSO DEMÜTIG AN DIE SACHE RANGEHEN UND BESSER EINEN SCHUSS ALKOHOL MEHR AN DIE PFLAUME.

ZUTATEN FÜR 4 FREUNDE:

25 g	Zucker
150 g	Trockenpflaumen
1	Zimtstange
1	Bio-Zitrone, Abrieb
	Don Papa Rum
1–2 TL	Stärke

FÜR DER REIS:

125 g	Milchreis
½ l	Milch
1	Vanilleschote
40 g	Zucker
1 Prise	Salz

UND MIT SCHMACKES:

Pflaumen 1 Stunde in Don Papa Rum baden lassen. Zitrone waschen und Schale abreiben. Die Trockenpflaumen mit dem Einweich-Rum in einem Topf gemeinsam mit Zimtstange, Zucker und Zitronenabrieb 20 Minuten köcheln lassen. Speisestärke mit etwas Wasser glattrühren und mit den Pflaumen binden.

Den Milchreis abspülen und mit 100 ml Wasser und einer Prise Salz einmal aufkochen lassen. Nun Milch, Vanillemark und Zucker dazugeben und 45 Minuten bei kleiner Flamme quellen lassen.

Gemeinsam servieren und in glückliche Gesichter schauen ...

„BRIKETTS AUF NEUSCHNEE"
KINDERESSEN, IS' KLAR,
KENNSTE! IS' ABER WIE IN DER
WERBUNG: MACHT DIE BLAGEN
FROH UND MALOCHER
EBENSO – VOR ALLEM MIT
RUM!

NACHTISCH

Zimtmöhre
SCHLAPPOHR

HATTU MÖHRCHEN, MUTTU ZIMT DRAUF TUN!

ZUTATEN FÜR 4 PORTIONEN:

200 g	Karotten
	brauner Zucker
1 TL	Zimt
	Kreuzkümmel
	Sesamsaat, weiß und schwarz
1 EL	Butter
	Salz/Pfeffer

UND BITTE ...

Karotten schälen und in Scheiben schneiden. Im Topf 10 Min bissfest garen. Anschließend in der Pfanne mit Butter und Zucker anbraten und karamellisieren lassen. Mit Zimt und Kümmel abschmecken und in Sesam schwenken.

Gesund ist es allemal, Geschmacksexplosion kann's auch. Und rein optisch? Ja, Burner!

Rote-Beete-Tatar Recklinghausen mit Ziegenkäse

EINFACH MAL AUF SICH WIRKEN LASSEN …

ZUTATEN FÜR 4 PORTIONEN:

400 g Rote Beete, vorgegart
1 Ziegenkäserolle
4 TL brauner Rohrzucker

FÜR DIE MARINADE:

2 EL Walnussöl
2 TL rotes Johannisbeergelee
4 TL Löwensenf, Bio Dijon
4 Stiele Dill
Salz/Pfeffer

Flammenwerfer zum Karamellisieren

UND ACTION:

Rote Beete in Stücke schneiden. Die Marinade aus Walnussöl, Johannisbeergelee, Salz, Pfeffer, Löwensenf und Dill verrühren. Über das Rote-Beete-Tatar geben und ziehen lassen.

Von der Ziegenrolle kleine Taler abschneiden und auf das Tatar geben. Braunen Zucker drauf-streuen und mit dem Flammenwerfer karamel-lisieren.

Macht sich gut auf Spinat als Unterlage oder an Feldsalat.

Achtung! Bitte dieses Gericht nicht im Freien zubereiten. Waldbrandgefahr! Danke.

Gurkensalat EMSCHER mit saurer Sahne, im Glas

DARF AUF KEINER FAMILIENFEIER FEHLEN, ODER EINEM PICKNICK FÜR ZWEI ...

ZUTATEN FÜR 2 VERLIEBTE:

½	Salatgurke
1 Becher	saure Sahne
½	Zitrone, Saft
einige Stängel Dill	
1 Prise	Zucker
	Salz/Pfeffer

SO GEHT'S:

Salatgurke schälen, entkernen und würfeln. 10 Minuten stehen lassen, damit es Wasser zieht. Das Wasser abgießen, dafür die saure Sahne dazu. Die Dillspitzen abzupfen, fein hacken und hineingeben, dann das Ganze mit Zitronesaft, Salz, Pfeffer und Zucker abschmecken.

Nur Verlieben müsst ihr euch schon alleine ...

Gemüsefrikadelle Grünschnabel

MIT MINZ-DIP! SEHR COOL, SEHR MINZIG – EIN FRISCHEKICK!

ZUTATEN FÜR 4 PORTIONEN:

500 g	Gemüse (Karotten, Kohlrabi, Fenchel, Sellerie, Brokkoli, Pastinaken, Steckrübe, etc. – wenn's mal schnell gehen muss, tut es natürlich auch TK-Gemüse)
¼ l	Gemüsebrühe
1	Ei
4 EL	Haferflocken
100 g	Semmelbrösel
	Kräutermischung: Kerbel, Schnittlauch, Petersilie, Liebstöckel, etc.
3 EL	Pflanzenöl

FÜR DEN DIP:

2oo g	Joghurt, 10 % Fett
4 Stiele	Minze
etwas	Zitronensaft
1 Prise	Zucker
	Salz/Pfeffer

AUF GEHT'S:

Gemüse mit einem Stabmixer pürieren und mit dem Ei, der Gemüsebrühe, den Haferflocken und den fein gehackten Kräutern vermengen. Kleine Frikadellen formen, in den Semmelbröseln wälzen und etwa eine halbe Stunde kalt stellen. Anschließend mit etwas Pflanzenöl von beiden Seiten braten.

Für den Dip: Minze fein hacken und mit dem Joghurt verrühren. Salz, Pfeffer, etwas Zitronensaft und 'ne Prise Zucker runden das Ganze ab.

SCHREBER-GARTEN

SCHREBBERGARTEN, LAUBE, GERNE TAUBENZUCHT, STÜCKSKEN GARTEN UND ICH SACH MA … FREIHEIT. GRILL ANWERFEN, WÜRSTCHEN DRAUF, KINDER INS PLANSCHBECKEN WERFEN, PLAUSCH MIT DEN NACHBARN, PÜLLEKEN INNE HAND UND VOR ALLEM „MENSCH BLEIBEN“, WIE SCHON DER TEGTMEIER

Pochiertes Ei SCHIMANSKI mit Speck

ZUTATEN FÜR 2 PORTIONEN:

2	Eier
2 Scheiben	westfälischer Schinkenspeck
3 EL	Crème fraîche leger
1	Avocado
2 Stängel	Petersilie
1 EL	Essig
1	frisches Brötchen
	Salz/Pfeffer/Paprika, edelsüß

LEICHT UND FIX:

Salzwasser mit dem Essig zum Kochen bringen. Parallel kleine Pfanne erhitzen und Frühstücksspeck darin kross anbraten. Die Crème fraîche mit Paprika verrühren, Avocado halbieren, Kern raus, dann und in Scheiben schneiden.

Eier in 2 Tassen gleiten lassen und die Hitze vom Essigwasser runterdrehen, bis es spiegelglatt ist. Mit einer Gabel einen Strudel erzeugen und das Ei hineingleiten lassen. Etwa 4 Minuten kochen. Mit einer Schaumkelle herausnehmen und das zweite Ei zubereiten.

Jetzt wird geschichtet: Unten liegt die Brötchenhälfte, Avocadoscheiben folgen. Jetzt kommt das Ei ins Spiel, gefolgt von der Paprika-Crème. Der Speck vollendet, mit der Petersilie als schmückendem Beiwerk. Salz, Pfeffer – was für eine akrobatische Gesamtleistung. Vorhang!

Dreierlei gefüllte Eier
Vatter Morgana

ZUTATEN FÜR 10 GEFÜLLTE EIERHÄLFTEN:

5	Eier
1 EL	Löwensenf, Bio Dijon
1 TL	Weißweinessig
60 g	Crème fraîche
60 g	Joghurt, 10 % Fett
	Salz/Pfeffer

SCHNITTLAUCH-SCHINKEN-EIER (A 40):

1 EL	Schnittlauch
30 g	Schinken

LACHS-DILL-EIER (A 43):

30 g	Lachs
1 TL	Dill

SARDELLEN-OLIVEN-EIER (A 46):

30 g	schwarze Oliven
2	Sardellen
1 EL	Kapern

SO LÄUFT'S AB:

Eier in kochendes Wasser geben und 10–12 Minuten kochen, kalt abschrecken und pellen.

Nun zur Füllung: Eier halbieren, das Eigelb herauslöffeln und mit Crème fraîche, Joghurt, Essig und Löwensenf glatt verrühren. Mit Salz und Pfeffer abschmecken und in drei Portionen aufteilen.

Für die A 40 (Schnittlauch-Schinken): Schinken kleinschneiden, Schnittlauch in feine Röllchen schneiden, eine Handvoll zurückbehalten, den Rest unter die Basismasse mischen.

Für die A 43 (Lachs-Dill): Lachs kleinschneiden, Dill hacken. Einen Teil beiseitestellen, den Rest unter die Grundmasse mischen.

Für die A 46 (Sardellen-Oliven-Kapern): Die drei Zutaten fein schneiden. Etwa die Hälfte unter die Eigelbmasse mischen. Der Rest bleibt als Topping zurück.

Die drei Eigelbmassen jeweils in einen Spritzbeutel füllen und die Eihälften damit befüllen. Danach Schnittlauch-Schinken auf die A 40, Dill-Lachs auf die A 43 und Sardellen, Oliven, Kapern auf die A 46 streuen.

Bitte nur zuhause und nicht auf öffentlichen Straßen oder Autobahnen zubereiten!

Senfeier OBERHAUSEN im Glas

VIELLEICH DAS BESTE, WAS EINEM EI PASSIEREN KANN: DAS WARME SENFBAD UND DIE BEGEGNUNG MIT DEM GUT ERZOGENEN SPINAT. SCHON FÜR DIE OPTIK GIBT'S 'NEN PREIS.

ZUTATEN FÜR 4 GLÄSER:

4 Eier

FÜR DIE SENFSAUCE:

2 EL	Löwensenf Extra
1	Schalotte
50 ml	Milch
50 ml	Sahne
150 ml	Gemüsebrühe
20 g	Mehl
20 g	Butter
1 Prise	Zucker
1 TL	Curry
	Salz/Pfeffer

FÜR DEN SPINAT:

150 g	Spinat
1	Schalotte
10 g	Butter

MACH MA' SO:

Für die Senfsauce: Schalotte klein würfeln und in Butter andünsten. Mehl und Currypulver einstreuen und verrühren. Brühe, Sahne und Milch dazu und einmal aufkochen lassen. 5 Minuten bei kleiner Hitze köcheln lassen. Danach mit Salz, Pfeffer, Löwensenf und Zucker abschmecken.

Die Eier 6 Minuten kochen, kalt abschrecken und pellen.

Für den Spinat: Schalotte klein würfeln und mit dem gewaschenen Spinat in etwas Butter andünsten. 5 Minuten köcheln lassen und mit Salz und Pfeffer würzen.

In die Weckgläser zuerst den Spinat, dann die Senfsauce und final zur Krönung die Eier platzieren. Mit etwas Löwensenf krönen – Augenweide!

EIERSPEISEN

Bierfrikadelle Wedau

„ICH HÄTTE GERN EIN BRÖTCHEN ZUR FRIKADELLE."

„IST SCHON DRIN."

„DANN BITTE NOCH EIN BRÖTCHEN."

„IST AUCH SCHON DRIN."

ZUTATEN FÜR 8 FRIKOS:

200 g	Rinderhack
200 g	Bratwurstbrät
1	Zwiebel
1	Ei
1	Brötchen, vom Vortag
1 Flasche	König Pilsener
½	Bund Petersilie
	Salz/Pfeffer
1 EL	Löwensenf Extra
2 EL	Pflanzenöl

SO GEHT'S:

Das altbackene Brötchen in eine Schüssel geben, mit König Pilsener übergießen und einweichen lassen. Die Zwiebel schälen, klein hacken und in Öl glasig dünsten. Petersilie hacken und mit der gedünsteten Zwiebel vermischen und mit Rinderhack und Wurstbrät hinein in die Schüssel. Außerdem Löwensenf und das Ei dazu und mit Salz und Pfeffer würzen.

Nun wird die ganze Masse schön verknetet, bis sie geschmeidig und glatt ist und ruht dann eine Stunde im Kühlschrank.

Frikomasse mit angefeuchteten Händen zu acht Frikadellen formen und mit etwas Öl bei mittlerer Hitze von beiden Seiten braten.

Dazu passt Gurkensalat als auch Kartoffelsalat. Haben wir ja im Programm ...

Löwensenf
EXTRA

Fischfrikadelle FISCHKOPP mit Granatapfel-Dip

FISCH TRIFFT ORIENT, NORDSEE MEETS BOSPORUS ...

EINKAUFSZETTEL FÜR 4 PORTIONEN:

400 g	Fischfilet
1	Brötchen, vom Vortag
1 Bund	Kräuter (Petersilie, Dill, Schnittlauch etc.)
1	Zwiebel
1	Ei
	Salz/Pfeffer
4 EL	Pflanzenöl

FÜR DEN DIP:

100 g	Granatapfelkerne
1 EL	Granatapfelsaft
	Joghurt, 10 % Fett
	Salz/Pfeffer

ABLAUFPLAN:

Zwiebel klein würfeln und Brot in kleine Stücke schneiden. Das Fischfilet zerteilen und zusammen mit dem Ei zu einer nicht zu feinen Masse verarbeiten. 12 Frikadellen formen und 30 Minuten kaltstellen.

Öl in einer großen Pfanne erhitzen und die Fischfrikadellen bei mittlerer Hitze von jeder Seite etwa 4–5 Minuten braten.

Für den Dip den Granatapfelsaft und ganze Granatapfelkerne mit dem Joghurt verrühren und mit Salz und Pfeffer abschmecken.

DUISBURG - RUHRORT ... HOLLÄNDISCHE KÜSTE WÜRDE MAN AUCH GLAUBEN, ODER?

Apfel-Birnen-Frikadelle Schrebbergarten

ÄH ... MIT CURRY-SENF-KREUZKÜMMEL-DIP? GENAU!

ZUTATEN FÜR 8 FRIKOS:

400 g	Rinderhack
1	Brötchen, mindestens von gestern
1	Apfel
1	Birne
1	Schalotte
1	Ei
2 EL	Pflanzenfett

FÜR DEN DIP:

1 EL	Zitronensaft
200 g	saure Sahne
	Salz/Pfeffer/Curry/ Paprikapulver/Kreuzkümmel
1 EL	Löwensenf Extra

SO WIRD'S GEMACHT:

Das olle Brötchen wird eingeweicht, Apfel und Birne werden geschält und in kleine Stücke geschnitten. Schalotte ebenso.

Das Hack mit Ei, Schalottenwürfeln und Brötchen mischen und massieren. Sie lieben das. Dann Apfel- und Birnenstücke dazu und nach weiterer Massage acht kleine Frikadellen kneten und beidseitig etwa 4–5 Minuten im Pflanzenfett braten.

Die saure Sahne mit Zitronensaft, Curry, Kreuzkümmel, Paprikapulver und Löwensenf verrühren und mit Salz und Pfeffer abschmecken. Guten Appetit!

100 %
NATÜRLICHE

FRIKADELLEN

BREMSKLOTZ, TÜRSTOPPER, FRIKADÖSE, BAUARBEITERPRALINE … OMMAS FRIKO, „KNUTSCHKUGEL“ … HERRLICH GEFÄHRLICH …

ZUM HOCKER
ZUM HOCKER
ZUM HOCKER
ZUM HOCKER

Matjes-Hering-Trilogie Deichgraf

ZUTATEN FÜR 4 PORTIONEN:

200 g	Matjes
100 g	Rote Beete
1	rote Zwiebel
2	Äpfel
	Salz/Pfeffer
	ja, und natürlich Spieße, die das Gebilde zusammenhalten

SO WIRD ES GUT:

Rote Beete, Matjesfilet und Äpfel in quadratische Stücke schneiden, die Zwiebel schälen, die Enden abschneiden, halbieren und die einzelnen Schichten trennen. Das Ganze übereinander stapeln und mit Holzspießen bei Laune und auf Position halten. Pfeffer und Salz auf die Rote Beete streuen. Finito la musica ...

WIE,
DAT IS SPIEßIG?
ICH HELF DIR GLEICH
MAL, DU VOGEL.

Matjes-Kartoffel Villa Hügel

„HEUT' MITTACH GIBBET FEINSTE PELLMÄNNER MIT MATJES."

EINKAUFSKORB FÜR 4 ESSER:

2	Matjesfilets
400 g	kleine Kartoffeln/Drillinge
200 g	Frischkäse
etwas	Schnittlauch
1 Prise	Zucker
	Salz/Pfeffer/Chilipulver
½	Bio-Zitrone, Saft

ARBEITSPLATTE:

Die kleinen Kartoffeln gut abwaschen und mit Pelle etwa 20 Minuten garkochen. Gabelprobe! Halbieren und auf der Unterseite etwas abschneiden, damit die Hälften standfest sind.

Frischkäse mit Salz, Pfeffer, Chilipulver und etwas Zitronensaft abschmecken. Jetzt kommen die Matjesstücke auf die Creme und Schnittlauchröllchen als Garnitur on Top. Fertig!

König Pilsener
PURUM LAUDATUR
NACH DEM REINHEITSGEBOT
1516
Heute ein König

Gurke-Lachs-Häppchen Uschi

DAT MACHT ABER MAL WAT HER! GEHT AUCH MIT FORELLE ODER HERING ...

EINKAUF FÜR 4:

100 g	Räucherlachs
½	Salatgurke
200 g	körniger Frischkäse
1 El	Zitrone
1 Bund	Schnittlauch
1 Bund	Dill
½ Bund	Petersilie
	Salz/Pfeffer

PASS AUF!

Räucherlachs würfeln und mit Zitronensaft, Schnittlauchröllchen, Dill, Petersilie zum Frischkäse geben. Mit Salz und Pfeffer abschmecken und cremig rühren.

Salatgurke waschen und die Enden abschneiden, dann halbieren und längs teilen. Mit einem Löffel die Kerne entfernen, dann die Creme in die Gurke geben und mit etwas Dill und Schnittlauch garnieren. Biddeschön!

Matjestatar
HALDE HANIEL

WENN'S GUT AUSSIEHT, SIEHT'S GUT AUS ... MATJES, APFEL, ZWIEBEL, RADIESCHEN, GURKE ... PUMPERNICKEL - EIN GEMÄLDE, EIN STILLLEBEN, ALTE HOLLÄNDISCHE MEISTER EBEN!

ZUTATEN FÜR 4:

4 Scheiben	Pumpernickel
2	Matjesfilets
1	Gewürzgurke
1	Apfel
2	Zwiebeln
1 TL	Olivenöl
1 Spritzer	Zitronensaft
1 EL	Dill
1 EL	Schnittlauch
	Pfeffer/Chilipulver

SO GEHT'S:

Matjes, Gurke und Apfel würfeln. Schnittlauch in Röllchen schneiden, Dill und Zwiebeln hacken. Zwiebeln kurz in etwas Öl andunsten.

Das ganze Gedöns mit Olivenöl, Zitronensaft, Pfeffer und Chilipulver mischen und durchziehen lassen. Eine Scheibe Pumpernickel in einen passenden Servierring geben oder ggf. ausstechen. Mit dem Matjestatar auffüllen, leicht andrücken und Ende Gelände.

Eine Zitronenscheibe als Deko und einige Schnittlauchröllchen machen natürlich einen schlanken Fuß.

König Pilsener

Matjeshappen Kokoschinski

ZUTATEN FÜR 4:

4	Matjesfilets
1	Apfel
3	Gewürzgurken
1	kleine Zwiebel
½	Zitrone, Saft und Abrieb
2 EL	Löwensenf, süß
1 TL	Zucker
1 EL	Meerrettich
1 EL	Öl
	Pfeffer

SO LÄUFT'S:

Matjes in kleine Häppchen schneiden. Zwiebel schälen und fein hacken, Gewürzgurken klein schneiden. Apfel schälen, Kerngehäuse entfernen und in kleine Stücke schneiden. Alles in eine Schüssel geben.

Für die Marinade Zitronensaft, Löwensenf und Pfeffer verrühren und dazugeben. Nach Geschmack evtl. 'ne Prise Zucker beigeben. Alles schön miteinander vermischen und zwei Stunden im Kühlschrank ziehen lassen.

Dazu passen Pellkartoffeln, die Kräcker oder auch die Kohleklumpen. Oder einfach so …

DER KEMNADER SEE BEI WITTEN. VON WEGEN, DAT RUHRGEBIET IS' GRAU. NACHTS VIELLEICHT, DU HEIOPEI. DIESER RUHRSTAUSEE MIT EINEM 8 KM LANGEN RUNDWEG WURDE 1979 FERTIGGESTELLT UND IST EINE GRÜNE OASE VOR DEN TOREN BOCHUMS.

FISCH MUSS SCHWIMMEN...

Die Fischvielfalt ist im Ruhrgebiet überschaubar. Der Matjes ist ein junger Hering, der noch nicht geschlechtsreif ist und alles noch vor sich hat. Und der Hering ist einfach ein Hering und geschlechtsreif. Gut, wenigstens darf er sich Bismarkhering nennen, wenn auch nicht „von Bismark". Die Forelle und der Lachs bereichert die Pottküche sicher auch noch, aber dann wird es schon eng.

Wenngleich das Revier nicht am Meer liegt, hätte es doch Chancen, eine riesige Seenplatte zu werden, wenn nicht Pumpen es dauerhaft trocken halten würden. Geborgtes Land. Der Bergbau hat es tiefergelegt, teilweise um über 20 Meter. Bis unter den Grundwasserspiegel. Fast ein Fünftel des Ruhrpotts stünden dann unter Wasser. Jährlich kostet die Trockenlegung einen dreistelligen Millionenbetrag.

... aber das nur nebenbei ... die Matjeshappen drängeln schon ...

Kartoffeltaler Eishockey-Puck

DIE SPORTLICHE ANTWORT AUF DEN GUTEN ALTEN KARTOFFELPUFFER – UND DER WAR JA SCHON IMMER EINE BANK. SOZUSAGEN STAMMSPIELER, KEIN BANKDRÜCKER.

DAT BRAUCHSTE FÜR VIER:

500 g	Kartoffeln
1	Ei
150 g	Mehl
1 El	Crème fraîche
	Muskat
½ TL	Salz
1 EL	Majoran
1 EL	Schnittlauch
8 EL	Butter oder Pflanzenmargarinecreme

MACH ET:

Kartoffeln 20–25 Minuten in Salzwasser weichkochen, dann durch die Presse drücken oder stampfen. Crème fraîche, Mehl, Salz, Muskat und Ei vermischen. Die Kräuter hacken und ebenfalls untermischen. Gut verkneten, bis ein glatter, geschmeidiger Teig entstanden ist. Den Teig zu einer Rolle formen und in Taler schneiden.

In Butter oder Öl von beiden Seiten knusprig braten. Sieht gut aus, ist gut drauf und kann man als Unterlage für Dillcreme mit Räucherlachs nehmen. Oder einfach so ...

Kräuter-Kartoffel-Eier-Salat Maikönigin

DAS IST JA WOHL AUCH MAL 'NE ANSAGE ... EIN GEMÄLDE GERADEZU! DA KANN MAN MAL RICHTIG BEI DER SCHWIEGERMUTTER PUNKTEN!

ZUTATEN FÜR 4 PORTIONEN:

1 kg	Kartoffeln, festkochend
6	Eier
2 TL	Löwensenf Extra
3 EL	Zitronensaft
100 g	Joghurt, 10 % Fett
100 g	frische Kräuter für grüne Sauce (Petersilie, Dill, Kerbel, Estragon, Sauerampfer, Schnittlauch, Liebstöckel etc.)
150 ml	Gemüsebrühe
6 EL	Pflanzenöl
1 Prise	Zucker
	Salz/Pfeffer
	Rosenpaprika, scharf
½	Rote Beete
	Feldsalat

SO WIRD'S GEMACHT:

Die Kartoffeln waschen und 25 Minuten in gesalzenem Wasser kochen. Gleichzeitig die Eier hart kochen, abschrecken und vierteln. Die Kartoffeln abgießen, abkühlen lassen, pellen und in Scheiben von 0,8 cm schneiden. War'n Witz!

Die Kräuter klein schneiden und mit Joghurt, Löwensenf, Zitronensaft, Brühe und dem Pflanzenöl pürieren. Anschließend mit Salz, Pfeffer, Zucker und dem Paprikapulver abschmecken.

Finale: Eier, Kartoffeln und die Kräuter werden in einer großen Schüssel gemischt, umarmen sich und schließen Freundschaft. Nehmt euch ein Beispiel! Die Rote Beete in feine Streifen schneiden und mit dem Feldsalat mischen. Kartoffeln und Eier dürfen dann dekorativ auf dem Salat herumliegen.

Zitroniger Kartoffelsalat Baldeneysee

MANN, SIEHT DAS GUT AUS! EINFACH, SCHNELL, ABER EINE WUCHT!

ZUTATEN FÜR 4 PORTIONEN:

800 g	Kartoffeln

DRESSING:

1 TL	Löwensenf Extra
4 EL	Crème fraîche
100 g	Joghurt
1 Bund	Schnittlauch
1 EL	Zitronensaft
1 EL	Zitronenabrieb
	Salz/Pfeffer

RAN AN DIE KARTOFFELN:

Kartoffeln waschen und ungeschält 25–30 Minuten in Salzwasser kochen. Anschließend in Scheiben schneiden.

Für das Dressing den Schnittlauch in feine Röllchen schneiden, dann alle Zutaten verrühren und mit Salz und Pfeffer abschmecken. Die Kartoffelscheiben vorsichtig unter die Marinade heben und zu guter Letzt einige zurückbehaltene Ringe Schnittlauch zwanglos, aber dekorativ darüber streuen.

Grünkohl-serviettenknödel Graf Koks

DER SERVIETTENKNÖDEL, EIN GANZ FEINER HERR ... ÜBRIGENS PASST ER GANZ HERVORRAGEND ZUR FRAU PFEFFERPOTTHAST!

ZUTATEN FÜR 4 PERSONEN:

200 g	Laugenbrezeln vom Vortag
2	Eier
400 ml	Milch
200 g	Grünkohl, TK oder frisch (gut ausdrücken)
1	Muskat/Salz/Pfeffer
8	Siedewürste, nach Geschmack Löwensenf Extra

SCHRITT FÜR SCHRITT:

Laugenbrezel klein schneiden, Eier und Milch verquirlen. Alles in eine Schüssel geben und vermengen und mit Muskat, Salz und Pfeffer würzen. Fast hätte ich es verschwitzt: die Zwiebeln dazugeben und den ausgedrückten Grünkohl natürlich! Vermengen und ruhen lassen. Pssst!

Nach 20 Minuten wecken. Alufolie ausbreiten, darüber Klarsichtfolie legen und die Knödelmasse darauf ausbreiten. Zusammenrollen und die Enden wurstartig verdrehen. Ja, is 'ne Bastelarbeit!

In kochendem Wasser 20 Minuten ziehen lassen. Knödelwurst rausnehmen und in Scheiben schneiden. Man kann sie leicht in Butter anbraten bis sie leicht bräunlich sind. Muss man aber nicht.

Und zur Wurst natürlich unbedingt Löwensenf!

WENNSSE LECKER WILLS, GEH BEI DIE OMMA ODER ANNE BUDE.

PURUM LAUDATUR
König Pils

Pfefferpotthast
HASTA LA VISTA

EIN MUSS DER WESTFÄLISCHEN KÜCHE, DAS GULASCH DES WESTENS – WÄRMT, MACHT GLÜCKLICH UND GANZ WICHTIG: SANFTMÜTIG! GERNE ETWAS ROTWEIN, NICHT NUR INS GERICHT ...

ZUTATEN FÜR 4 PORTIONEN:

4	Zwiebeln
1 kg	Rindergulasch
1,2 l	Rinderfond
1 Flasche	König Pilsener
1 Schuss	Rotwein
2 EL	Kapern
1 EL	Mehl
3	Lorbeerblätter
8	Pimentkörner
3	Wacholderbeeren
	Pfeffer, grün und schwarz
	Salz
1	Bio-Zitrone, Zesten für die Deko
40 g	Schweineschmalz

AN DIE ARBEIT:

Die Zwiebeln schälen und in schmale Streifen schneiden.

Das Schweineschmalz in einem großen Topf erhitzen und das Rindergulasch bei starker Hitze anbraten. Die Zwiebeln dazugeben bis sie leicht gebräunt sind, dann mit dem Mehl bestäuben, anschwitzen und schließlich mit dem König Pilsener und Rotwein ablöschen. Etwas einkochen lassen, dann den Fond dazugeben. Jetzt die Kräuter hinein. Einmal hochkochen lassen und danach bei schwacher Hitze 2½ Stunden schmoren lassen.

Die Bio-Zitrone heiß abspülen, die Schale abreiben und den Saft einer halben Zitrone auspressen. Gleich is' fertig! Kapern, Zitronensaft, Zitronenabrieb, Pfeffer und etwas Salz geben den letzten Pfiff!

Westfälische Potthucke

HUCKE VOLL

KARTOFFELKUCHEN MIT FLEISCHEINLAGE. DER NAME BEDEUTET „WAS IM TOPF HOCKT". JA, DA KANN EBEN ALLES MÖGLICHE DRIN HOCKEN. ICH MACH' DAS MIT EINER METZGERBRATWURST UND WÜRZE MIT MAJORAN, MUSKATNUSS, SALZ UND PFEFFER. ORIGINAL KOMMEN DA METTENDEN REIN, ES KÖNNTE ABER AUCH WESTFÄLISCHER SCHINKEN SEIN ...

ZUTATEN FÜR 4 PERSONEN:

600 g	Kartoffeln
3	Eier
250 g	Crème fraîche
4	Bratwürste
	Salz/Pfeffer/Maskat/Majoran
etwas	Butter
etwas	Butterschmalz
	Löwensenf Extra

SO WIRD'S WAS:

Den Backofen auf 200 °C (Ober/Unterhitze) vorheizen.

Ein Drittel der Kartoffeln kochen und stampfen, den Rest schälen, roh reiben und anschließend beide Kartoffelmassen vermengen.

Die Crème fraîche mit den Eiern verquirlen und mit Pfeffer, Salz, etwas Muskat und Majoran würzen.

Eine Kastenbackform mit etwas Butter einfetten und die Hälfte der Kartoffelmasse hineingeben. Jetzt die Bratwürste auflegen und mit der übrigen Kartoffelmasse bedecken. Das Ganze etwa 50 Minuten backen.

Raus aus der Röhre, in Scheiben schneiden und mit etwas Butterschmalz von beiden Seiten leicht anbraten. Etwas Löwensenf dazu kann nicht schaden!

ZUM HOCKER
MARKUS KREBS
SCHMACKOFATZ!
Jägermeister
Ruhrpott

ZUM HOCKER

WILLKOMMEN!

Minischnitzel GLADBECK

KLEIN, KROSS, HANDLICH … PASST IN JEDE DAMENHANDTASCHE.

EINKAUF FÜR 4 LEUTE

500 g	Schweine-, Puten-, oder Kalbsschnitzel
150 g	Pankomehl oder Knäckebrot (Hauptsache knusprig)
1	Bio-Zitrone
50 g	Mehl
2	Eier
2 EL	Butterschmalz

ABLAUF

Knäckebrot schreddern. Zitrone heiß abwaschen, eine Hälfte fein abreiben, die andere Hälfte in Spalte schneiden. Zitronenschale mit Salz und Pfeffer unters Knäckegekrümel mischen.

Schnitzel flachdrücken und in Stücke (ca. 5 cm) schneiden. Salz, Pfeffer drüber.

Drei Schalen bereitstellen. Eine für Mehl, eine für das verquirlte Eiergebilde und eine für die Knäckepanade.

Die kleinen Schnitzel durch Mehl, Ei und Panade ziehen und die Knäckekrümel leicht andrücken. Butterschmalz in einer Pfanne erhitzen und die Schnitzel bei mittlerer Hitze etwa 2 Minuten von jeder Seite goldbraun braten.

Raus aus der Pfanne und auf Küchenpapier entfetten lassen. Mit den Zitronenspalten servieren.

Chicorée untereinander
Drunter und Drüber

DIE WURSTBEILAGE IST VARIABEL, ABER ALLES VIELLEICHT IM GLAS? ODER HINTER GLAS?

TYPISCH RUHRPOTT! WARUM KARTOFFELN MIT SALATBEILAGE? EINFACH MISCHEN!

EINKAUF FÜR VIER:

4	Chicorée
300 g	Kartoffeln
3	Zwiebeln
½ l	Milch
1	Zitrone
3 EL	Olivenöl
1 Prise	Zucker
	Salz/Pfeffer/Paprika, scharf oder Chilipulver
4	Bratwürste
1 EL	Butterschmalz
	Löwensenf Extra

GANZ EINFACH:

Kartoffeln schälen und in Salzwasser kochen. Abgießen und mit der heißen Milch stampfen.

Chicorée waschen, fein schneiden. Zwiebeln klein hacken und mit einer Marinade aus Öl, Zitrone, Salz und Pfeffer, Zucker und Chilipulver vermischen. Chicorée hinzugeben.

Kartoffeln und Chicoréegemisch vorsichtig vermengen. Übereinander und untereinander! Kuddelmuddel!

Die Bratwürste in Butterschmalz anbraten und zusammen mit dem „Drunter und Drüber“ und einem guten Klecks Löwensenf servieren!

WENN IHR KEINEN CHICORÉE BEKOMMT, KÖNNT IHR AUCH ENDIVIE NEHMEN.

100 ml
100%
NATÜRLICHE
ZUTATEN

Blutwurst in Portweinzwiebeln
Flönz in Schweröl

BLUTWURST IST JA NICHT JEDERMANNS SACHE ... BRATWUST ODER METTENDEN KÖNNEN IN DER SAUCE ABER AUCH SCHWIMMEN. UND JETZT WAS GANZ VERRÜCKTES: MAN KANN DIE „FLÖNZ" AUCH WEGLASSEN UND DIE PORTWEINZWIEBELN ALLEIN GENIEßEN.
UN GETZ KOMMS' DU!

ZUTATEN FÜR 4 LEUTE:

200 g	Blutwurst
200 ml	Portwein
100 g	kleine Zwiebeln
1 EL	Balsamicoessig
1 EL	Olivenöl
1 EL	Butter
	Pfeffer
1 Prise	Zucker
	Rosmarinzweige

SCHRITTE:

Zwiebeln schälen und in Ringe schneiden. Mit Zucker und Balsamico bei niedriger Temperatur im Öl karamellisieren lassen. Mit Portwein abschmecken, dann einkochen lassen bis es wie Schweröl aussieht, hoffentlich aber anders schmeckt.

Blutwurst in Scheiben schneiden und in Butter anbraten. Die Zwiebeln auf den Scheiben anrichten, mit etwas Rosmarin garnieren und pfeffern. Feddich!

Currywurst im Glas Grugapark

RUHRGEBIET OHNE CURRYWURST? GEHT JA GAR NICHT! DIE WURST-QUALITÄT MUSS STIMMEN UND DIE SAUCE SELBSTGEMACHT SEIN. NEBEN EINER GUTEN METZGERBRATWURST DARF ES AUCH JEDE ANDERE WURSTSORTE SEIN: GEFLÜGELWURST, RINDSWURST, KRÄUTERWURST, VEGETARISCHE WURST ETC. AM ENDE SIEGT UND DOMINIERT DIE SCHÄRFE DER SAUCE UND SO SOLL DAS JA AUCH SEIN, ODER?

ZUTATEN FÜR 4 GLÄSER:

4	Würste eurer Wahl
1	Zwiebel
400 g	passierte Tomaten
1 EL	Tomatenmark
1 TL	Zitronensaft
1 Spritzer	Worcestershiresauce
1 Prise	Zucker
1 TL	Paprikapulver
2 TL	Currypulver
1 TL	Kreuzkümmelpulver
	Salz/Pfeffer
1 TL	Raps- oder Sonnenblumenöl

SO GEHT'S

Zwiebel häuten und würfeln. In einer Pfanne 2 Minuten im Öl andünsten. Das Tomatenmark hinzugeben, mitdünsten und mit den passierten Tomaten ablöschen. Die Sauce mit Salz, Pfeffer, Currypulver, Paprikapulver und Kreuzkümmel bereichern und mit Hilfe der Worcestershire-sauce, dem Zitronensaft und dem Zucker über die geschmackliche Ziellinie bringen.

Nun sind die Würste dran: Sie werden angstfrei 8–10 Minuten in etwas Öl in der Pfanne ganzkörpergebräunt. Anschließend in Scheiben schneiden, auf Spieße stecken und die kessen Dinger mit Currypulver bestäuben. Sie lieben das!

Jetzt wird die wohltemperierte Sauce ins Glas gefüllt und die Wurstspieße folgen. Und wenn sie nicht gegessen wurden, baden sie noch heute.

– Ende –

Himmel und Erde „Förderturm"

HIMMEL MEINT DEN APFEL UND ERDE DEN ERDAPFEL, SPRICH DIE KARTOFFEL ... GUT, FEHLT NOCH DIE BLUTWURST. VON DER FARBE KÖNNTE ES DIE HÖLLE SEIN. DA MÖCHTE ICH MICH ABER NICHT FESTLEGEN. KENN' MICH MIT HÖLLE NICHT SO AUS ...

ZUTATEN FÜR 4 PORTIONEN:

250 g	Blutwurst
500 g	Kartoffeln, mehlig
500 g	Apfel
125 ml	Milch
50 g	Butter
	Muskatnuss/Salz/Pfeffer/Zimt
	Butterschmalz zum Anbraten

SO WIRD'S WAS:

Kartoffeln schälen, waschen und in grobe Stücke schneiden. In Salzwasser zugedeckt 20–25 Minuten kochen. Dann abgießen und im offenen Topf ausdampfen lassen und zu einem Püree stampfen. Nach und nach die Milch zugeben bis zur gewünschten Konsistenz. Butter ran und mit Salz, Pfeffer und Muskatnuss abschmecken.

Äpfel schälen und kleinschneiden und bei mittlerer Hitze zu einem Apfelmus kochen. Mit etwas Zimt abschmecken.

Blutwurst in Scheiben schneiden, von beiden Seiten anbraten und auf Küchenrolle legen – zwecks Entfettung.

Schön übereinander stapeln, erst Apfelmus, dann Kartoffelbrei und oben drauf die Blutwurst. Und wehe, die kippt um! Zur Strafe ein Glas Bier auf Ex! Rauf auf den Löffel!

BLUTWURST AUF'M LÖFFEL SIEHT ERSTMAL TOFTE AUS UND MIT SOWAT GEWINNEN ANDERE KOCHSENDUNGEN!

Speckpfannkuchen „Mama Markus“

GEHT ALS GRUNDLAGE ODER AUCH AM MORGEN DANACH ... KLEIN, FLACH, RUND UND HERZHAFT! DAS IST NICHT EINFACH NUR EIN REZEPT, DAS IST EIN ZEITDOKUMENT ...

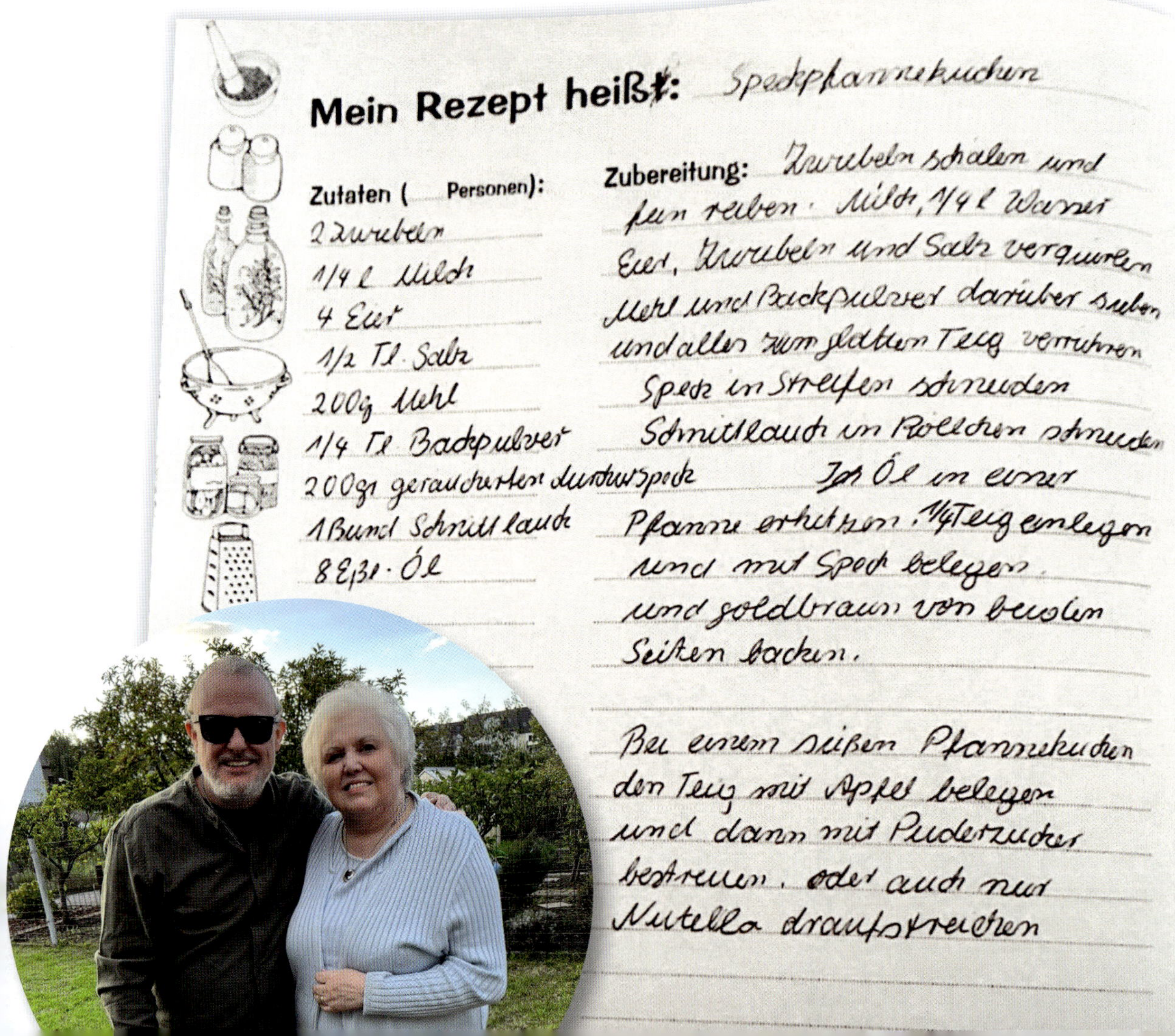

Mein Rezept heißt: Speckpfannekuchen

Zutaten (Personen):

2 Zwiebeln
1/4 l Milch
4 Eier
1/2 Tl. Salz
200g Mehl
1/4 Tl Backpulver
200gr geräucherten Durchwspeck
1 Bund Schnittlauch
8 Eßl. Öl

Zubereitung: Zwiebeln schälen und fein reiben. Milch, 1/4 l Wasser, Eier, Zwiebeln und Salz verquirlen. Mehl und Backpulver darüber sieben und alles zum glatten Teig verrühren. Speck in Streifen schneiden. Schnittlauch in Röllchen schneiden. ~~Ich~~ Öl in einer Pfanne erhitzen. 1/4 Teig einlegen und mit Speck belegen. und goldbraun von beiden Seiten backen.

Bei einem süßen Pfannkuchen den Teig mit Apfel belegen und dann mit Puderzucker bestreuen. oder auch nur Nutella draufstreichen

KLASSIKER

ZUM HOCKER
ZUM HOCKER
ZUM HOCKER
ZUM HOCKER
König

Pumpernickelklötzkes „Legoland“

ZUTATEN FÜR 4 PORTIONEN:

1 Pck.	Pumpernickel
400 g	Frischkäse
½ Bund	Schnittlauch
2 EL	Sahnemeerrettich
3–4	Kirschtomaten
	Salz/Pfeffer/Paprikapulver, edelsüß und Rosen, scharf

SO MACHEN WIR'S:

Pumpernickel in Quadrate schneiden. Tomaten pürieren und Schnittlauch in feine Ringe schneiden.

Den Frischkäse dritteln und jeweils in eine kleine Schüssel füllen. Eine für die Kräutercreme, eine für die Paprikacreme und eine für die Meerrettichcreme. Schnittlauch, Meerrettich und Tomate entsprechend verteilen und gut verrühren.

Mit Salz und Pfeffer würzen, nur die Paprikacreme bekommt sowohl mildes, als auch scharfes Paprikapulver, das Luder. Gut verrühren. Die Quadrate mit den Cremes bestreichen, anschließend aufeinandersetzen. Wie auf dem Foto.

Nicht direkt kochen, eher basteln. Glück auf!

Mettigelchen „Mettmann“

MEIN GOTT, DER METTIGEL ODER IN DIESEM FALL DAS IGELCHEN! VIELE SIND MIT IHM GROß GEWORDEN, ER IST KLEIN GEBLIEBEN. EIN POSSIERLICHES TIERCHEN, DAS AUF KEINER PARTY FEHLEN DURFTE, HALT EIN FEIERBIEST. IMMER EIN HINGUCKER. IMMER EIN RENNER ... WIE DER VW-KÄFER. LÄUFT UND LÄUFT UND LÄUFT ...

ZUTATEN FÜR 4 IGELFREUNDE (8 STÜCK):

8	Pumpernickel-Taler
200 g	Mett
½ Glas	Kapern
1	kleiner Rettich oder 2 Gewürzgurken
etwas	Löwensenf Extra
	Muskat/Salz/Pfeffer/Paprikapulver

BASTELANLEITUNG:

Das Mett würzen und daraus kleine, runde Kugeln formen, um sie dann in Igel zu verwandeln. Eine Igelschnauze modellieren und danach mit den Kapern die Augen und die Igelnase draufsetzen. Den Rettich oder die Gewürzgurken in kurze längliche Streifen schneiden und dem Igel ein Stachelkleid verpassen.

Die Pumpernickel-Taler mit einem Klecks Löwensenf versehen und die Igelchen darauf Platz nehmen lassen.

TIPP:

NATÜRLICH KÖNNT IHR AUCH ZWIEBELN IN LÄNGLICHE STREIFEN SCHNEIDEN, ABER DANN KÖNNT IHR NIEMANDEN MEHR KÜSSEN ... MUNDGERUCH MACHT JA BEKANNTLICH EINSAM. ICH HABE MICH FÜR EINEN KLEINEN WEISSEN, LEICHT SCHARFEN RETTICH ENTSCHIEDEN. RIECHT AUCH NICHT, HAT EINE LEICHTE SCHÄRFE ... SO, MEHR SAGE ICH JETZT NICHT.

König Pilsener

Pflaume im westfälischen Schinkenspeckmantel „Brikett“

ZUTATEN FÜR 8 „BRIKETTS“

100 g	Westfälischer Schinkenspeck
8	Trockenpflaumen, soft (ca. 100 g)
8	Salbeiblätter
1 Glas	Asbach Uralt

GEBRAUCHSANWEISUNG:

Die Pflaumen etwa eine Stunde in Asbach Uralt einlegen.

Anschließend mit den Salbeiblättern belegen und jeweils in eine Scheibe Schinkenspeck einwickeln.

In eine Porzellanform oder auf ein Backblech legen und im Backofen bei 200 °C (Ober/Unterhitze) 11 Min backen.

Zum Servieren auf Spieße stecken.

NE' SCHNELLE NUMMER, WÜRDE ICH MAL SAGEN. DAZU PASST IMMER EIN KLARER SCHNAPS ALS VERTEILER. ABER NACH JEDEM „BRIKETT“!

Kohlebrötchen „Grubengold“

TAGSÜBER ESSEN. IM DUNKELN FINDET MAN DIE GAR NICHT …
NUR DAS SCHARFE GEMÜSE LEUCHTET ROT UND GRÜN!

ZUTATEN FÜR 8 BRÖTCHEN:

300 g	Weizenmehl
200 ml	lauwarmes Wasser
1 TL	Salz
1 TL	Aktivkohle
1 TL	Trockenhefe
2	kleine milde Peperonischoten (aus dem Glas), rot und grün

AUF GEHT'S:

Hefe und Salz in lauwarmem Wasser auflösen und eine halbe Stunde gehen lassen.

Peperoni kleinschneiden und mit der Hefe-Salz-Mischung, Mehl und der Aktivkohle zu einem glatten Teig vermischen. 1 Stunde abgedeckt ruhen lassen.

Den Backofen auf 200 °C (Ober-/Unterhitze) vorheizen.

Den Teig aus der Schüssel nehmen, mit etwas Mehl bestreuen und daraus acht Brötchen formen. Auf der mittleren Schiene 25–30 Min backen und dann raus mit den Dingern!

Buchweizenkräcker „Krachmacher“

... LAUT, ABER EIN ECHTER KRACHER!

ZUTATEN FÜR REICHLICH KRACKER

350 g	Buchweizenmehl
1 TL	Meersalz
1	Ei
½ l	Wasser
2 EL	Olivenöl
1 TL	Rosenpaprika, scharf
	gesalzene Butter zum Einfetten

SO GEHT'S:

Den Backofen auf 200 °C (Umluft) vorheizen.

Mehl und Salz in eine Schüssel geben und ein Ei hineingeben. Das Wasser dazugeben und mit der Hand zu einem glatten Teig verarbeiten.

Eine beschichtete Pfanne mit gesalzener Butter einfetten und den Teig dünn verstreichen und bei mittlerer Hitze 2–3 Minuten von jeder Seite bräunen lassen. Herausnehmen und widerholen bis der Teig verbraucht ist.

Anschließend den Teig erst in Streifen und dann in Rauten schneiden. Die Rauten auf ein Backblech legen und im vorgeheizten Backofen 8–10 Minuten knusprig backen. Raus damit und auf Küchenpaper legen.

Dippen und es krachen lassen!

Kräuterdip „Vorgarten“

EINKAUFSKORB FÜR 4 PORTIONEN:

1 Bund	Petersilie
1 Bund	Rucola
4	Sardellen
1 Glas	Kapern
1	Gewürzgurke mit etwas Gurkenwasser aus dem Glas
1	altbackenes Brötchen
1 EL	Olivenöl
1 Spritzer	Zitrone
1 Prise	Zucker
	Pfeffer/Salz

SO WIRD'S GEFERTIGT:

Das Brötchen 15 Minuten einweichen. Petersilie und Rucola waschen, trockenschütteln und kleinhacken. Gewürzgurke in kleine Stücke hacken und zusammen mit Kapern und den kleingeschnittenen Sardellen hinzugeben. Einige Kapern als Topping aufheben. Schließlich das eingeweichte Brötchen gut ausdrücken und kleinzupfen und mit dem Olivenöl hinein ins Kräutervergnügen. Mit Zitronensaft, Salz, Pfeffer und einer Prise Zucker das Ganze abrunden.

Fertig! Frischer geht's nicht.

Makrelencreme Hafenmeisters Fensterkitt

ZUTATEN FÜR 4 PORTIONEN:

200 g	geräucherte Makrele
200 g	Joghurt, 10 % Fett
100 g	Crème fraîche
1 EL	Löwensenf, Bio Dijon
1 EL	Kapern
1	Orange
1 Spritzer	Worcestershiresauce
1 Schuss	Orangenlikör
	Meersalz/Pfeffer/Rosenpaprika

SO LÄUFT'S

Makrele mit der Gabel zerdrücken und mit Joghurt und Crème fraîche verrühren. Kapern, Orangesaft und -likör, Löwensenf und Worcestershiresauce dazugeben und mit den Gewürzen abschmecken. Mit Orangenscheiben dekorieren.

Nä, wat schön! Rauf auf den Tisch!

Matjescreme „Klabautermann“

ZUTATEN FÜR 4 PORTIONEN:

1	kleine Zwiebel
½	Apfel
200 g	Matjesfilet
1	Stange Staudensellerie
1	Gewürzgurke
½ Bund	Petersilie
½ Bund	Dill
½ Kästchen	Kresse
½	Bio-Zitrone (Abrieb)
200 g	Joghurt, 10 % Fett
etwas	Löwensenf Extra
	Salz/Pfeffer/Zucker

SO WIRD'S GEMACHT:

Zwiebel und Apfel schälen und kleinhacken.

Matjes, Sellerie und Gewürzgurke in kleine Würfel schneiden. Petersilie und Dill waschen und kleinschneiden.

Joghurt glattrühren und mit Zitronenabrieb, Löwensenf, Salz, Pfeffer und Zucker abgeschmeckt.
Kresse drauf, fertig!

Türöffner und Appetitanreger

SO 'NE TAPAS-SAUSE MUSS JA IRGENDWIE LOSGEHEN, ALSO STELLT MAN EIN PAAR DIPS AUF DIE THEKE ODER AUF DEN TISCH. „SO, SCHON MAL WAS VORWEG, BIS DIE TAPAS KOMMEN. WAS WOLLT IHR TRINKEN?“

REZEPTE

„DAT KRISSE AUFFE KETTE."

ICH SACH MA' SO:

Alle Rezepte sind einfach und leicht zu machen. Die Zutaten kriegt man überall und der Zeitaufwand ist überschaubar. Man will sich ja dem gepflegten Tresengespräch, den Gästen und natürlich den Getränken widmen. Anders gesagt, hier wird nicht das Rad neu erfunden und auch keins geschlagen. Es geht ums Essen, einfaches schmackhaftes Essen, das in die Region passt und zu den Leuten, die da leben. Fettich!

Natürlich arbeitet heute keiner mehr im Bergwerk, weniger Menschen am Hochofen, am Fließband oder auf dem Bau. Die Essgewohnheiten habe ich entsprechend weitestgehend den Rezepten angepasst ... Weniger Fett, weniger Zucker, kurzum weniger Kalorien und dennoch herzhaft.

Die Kalorien, die man beim Essen einspart, kann man dann großzügig bei den Getränken raushauen. Alles klar? Gut, dann legen wir los ...! Eins noch, die Rezepte sollen euch einladen, sie auszuprobieren und natürlich zu verändern und zu eurem ganz persönlichen Gericht zu machen. Es sind bloß Rezepte – Anregungen, nicht die Straßenverkehrsordnung ...

Lasset die Spiele beginnen!

EUER UDO

Ruhrpott
BRENNHOLZ VERLEIH

ZUM HOCKER
COMEDY-SHOWS, THEMENABENDE, LIVE-MUSIK – IM HOCKER IST IMMER WAT LOS!
SCHÖN, DASSE DA BIS'!
MITTEN IM POTT, IM HERZEN DUISBURGS LIEGT UNSERE VEREINSKNEIPE „ZUM HOCKER". GEMÜTLICHE HOLZVERKLEIDUNG, VOLLE THEKE, ARSCHKALTES KÖNIG PILSENER.
WIR FREUEN UNS AUF DEINEN BESUCH!

WILDES GRÜNES RUHRGEBIET!

SITZEN ZWEI KERLE AN DER THEKE VOR IHREM BIER UND STOßEN AN. SACHT DER EINE: „BOAH EH, SCHEIßTAG GEHABT, ICH HAB' GETZ NOCH SCHAUM VORM MUND."

SACHT DER ANDERE: „ECHT? BEI MIR IS GERADE ANDERSRUM." PROST!

mal vorwech

Essen is wichtig, Duisburg is wichtiger ... hömma, den kamma ma bringen ... nee getz ma ernsthaft, wat zwischen die Zähne, zum Kaun und Verdaun. Mal wat zum Pils, mal wat für die Seele und natürlich für'n Bauch. Daher ja auch dat Bauchgefühl. Kennt man ja gut, gerade im Ruhrpott.

So, pass auf, lecker musset sein und schmecken musset – is klar – „wie bei Mutta, Omma und man musset auch selber leicht zusammenfrickeln können. Schön wär auch, wenn's gut aussieht. Appetitlich sagt man ja auch oder ansprechend, schickobello eben. Weiss' wat ich mein' ...

ZUM HOCKER
PASS AUF ...
...RUHRPOTT-TAPAS MÜSSEN LECKER SCHMECKEN, GUT AUSSEHEN ... KLAR ...
...UND ZUM LECKER PILS PASSEN!
BEI FRAUEN ISSET ÄHNLICH, NÄ ..., KOMM ..., SCHERZ ...! DAT SCHNEIDN WIR RAUS ...!
„WENNSE NICH MEHR KANNS, MACH'N DECKEL."

Die Tapas

– EINE FAMILIE AUS SPANIEN –

Sie kommen aus Spanien, fühlen sich aber auch bei uns sehr wohl. Jeder kennt sie aus dem Spanienurlaub, wo sie sich auf der Theke rumlümmeln. Neben der Paella und dem Sangria-Eimer sind die Tapas sicherlich die beliebtesten kulinarischen Erinnerungen an die iberische Halbinsel, samt Inseln.

Natürlich vermissen die Tapas manchmal das Meer und die Sonne, aber sie sind sehr anpassungsfähig und gesellig, von daher im Ruhrgebiet bestens aufgehoben. „Tapa“ heißt übersetzt „Deckel“, wie Bierdeckel und der wurde einst von einem fürsorglichen spanischen Wirt auf das Wein- oder Bierglas der Gäste gelegt, um das kühlende kostbare Getränk vor waghalsigen Fliegen und anderen Insekten zu schützen. Auf den Deckel legte man zur Beschwerung zunächst einige Oliven und später auch noch eine Scheibe Brot. Beides hat der Gast dann in Windeseile verputzt. Der staunende Wirt legte weitere Köstlichkeiten auf den Deckel und der hocherfreute Gast bestellte noch ein Getränk, was wiederum den Wirt erfreute. So herrschte nun auf beiden Seiten der Theke große Freude und ganz nebenbei waren die Tapas erfunden.

„HOL MAL WAT FÜR AUF'N DUBBEL.“

HERR OBER, ICH MÖCHTE
ETWAS ESSEN. IRGENDWAS, WAS
SCHNELL GEHT, ICH MUSS GLEICH WEG."

„NEHMEN SIE DAS SCHNITZEL,
DAS MUSS AUCH WEG."

Willkommen in …

DAS RUHRGEBIET,

der Ruhrpott, oder kurz „der Pott“ ist mit etwa 5,1 Millionen Einwohnern der größte Ballungsraum Deutschlands und der viertgrößte Europas. Das ist doch mal eine Ansage. Außerdem gab es im Ruhrgebiet schon „Multikulti“, da glaubte man im Rest der Republik noch, es handele sich dabei um 'ne Küchenmaschine.

Der Pott ist aber schon lange kein Kohlenpott mehr, am 21. Dezember 2018 machte die letzte Zeche in Bottrop die Tür zu und damit endete die Ära des Untertageabbaus im Ruhrgebiet. Dennoch werden der Bergmann, seine Zeche und die Kohle immer zu dieser Region gehören und Kulturgut bleiben. Industriekultur klingt so menschenleer, ist es aber gar nicht. Damals nicht und heute auch nicht. Mit dem Ende der Kohle kam auch die Schließung vieler Stahlwerke und eine Region musste sich neu erfinden. Neu erfinden? Sowas kann der Ruhrpottler, das muss man dem nicht zweimal sagen. Das ist wie das Motto der Schalke-Fans: „Hinfallen kann man – aufstehen muss man!“

Heutzutage sind Zechen zu Kulturzentren geworden, Museen, Theater, Veranstaltungshallen etc. befinden sich in den alten Waschkauen, unter Fördertürmen und in ehemaligen Fabrikanlagen. Wo früher malocht wurde, wird heute getanzt, gespielt, musiziert und eben auch gegessen.

Esskultur ist eben auch Kultur, spiegelt es doch die Menschen einer Region wider, ihre Arbeit, ihre Gewohnheiten, ihre Leidenschaft und ihre Lebensfreude. In diesem Sinne, auf ins Ruhrgebiet. Ran an den Speck, ab in die Küche, rein in den Schrebergarten und nimm Platz am Tresen. Kein Fußballspiel ohne Stadionwurst mit Pils. Kein Sonntagsessen bei Omma ohne Kartoffelpuffer mit Apfelmus.

GLÜCK AUF!

Schön isset auch anderswo, aber nich' so wie hier.

ETWAS SCHÖNERES KANN MAN ÜBER SEINE HEIMAT KAUM SAGEN. DER RUHRPOTTLER SAGT UND MEINT DAS ABER SO, WEIL ES EBEN AUCH SEIN RUHRGEBIET, SEIN POTT IST UND BLEIBT. WER'S NICHT SCHÖN FINDET, MUSS VIELLEICHT GENAUER HINSCHAUEN UND MAL EINE ZEIT LANG DORT BLEIBEN.

VORWORT

Ein fröhliches ¡Olé! an alle Tapas-Liebhaberinnen und an die charmanten Señores, die im Anschluss die Rechnung bezahlen. „Tapa" bedeutet übersetzt „Deckel", und dieser wird mit Freude nach so einem Abend bezahlt, da man beim Tapas-Essen nicht nur jeden Moment, sondern auch jedes Tapa genossen hat. Wenn Fußball die schönste Nebensache der Welt ist, dann sind Tapas die schönste Kleinigkeit der Welt.

Sicherlich fragt sich der eine oder andere: warum Ruhrpott-Tapas?! Erstens mal finde ich, dass das Ruhrgebiet eine spannende und abwechslungsreiche Küche zu bieten hat, die Tapas-Variante ermöglicht es unseren Gästen, in kleinen Portionen die ganze Vielfalt des Ruhrgebietes zu erschmecken.

Gäbe es eine kulinarische Autobiografie von mir – sie würde wohl „Nicht aufgegessen" heißen. Ich bin einfach immer so schnell satt – weil ich während des Essens meistens so viel erzähle. Das Gelaber meinerseits macht es schwierig, ein Tellergericht von normaler Größe zu essen, bevor es kalt ist. Deshalb liebe ich es, mal hier und mal da kleine Portionen zu essen und wenn Tapas auf dem Tisch stehen, bin ich in meiner Genusswelt! Lecker, labern und lustig sein! Und ich kann am Abend meine eigenen Kreationen zusammenstellen: Matjes als Erstes, dann ein paar Gladbecker Minischnitzel und auch noch Schimanski-Ei mit Speck, warum nicht?!

Ich mag es „scharf und zack" – Löwensenf Extra auf meinen Appetithappen und mein Tag ist perfekt. Und König Pilsener ist bei mir ein Muss! Weil ich es darf. Es ist meine Kreation. Dem Weintrinker sei es vergönnt, diese leckeren Kleinigkeiten mit der Traube seiner Wahl zu feiern.

Ich liebe dieses Koch-Buch und danke insbesondere unserem wunderbaren Autor Udo Thies. Er ist mit sehr viel Herzblut in die Küche meiner Heimat eingetaucht und hat aus zahlreichen Klassikern großartige und zeitgemäße Tapas-Varianten entwickelt, bei denen zum Teil sogar Spirituosen wie Asbach Uralt und Don Papa Rum verwendet werden. Das Ergebnis ist einfach Weltklasse!

Probiert die Rezepte aus und findet dabei euren eigenen Tapas-Weg!

Und wer weiß, wer einem auf diesem so wohlschmeckenden Weg noch alles begegnet.

EUER MARKUS

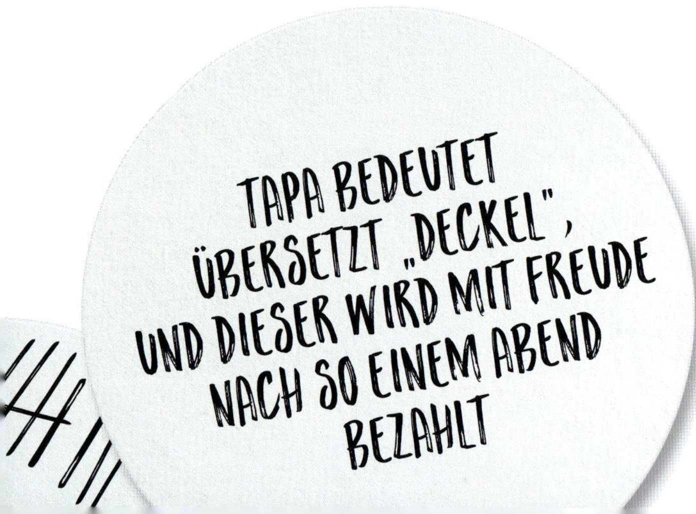

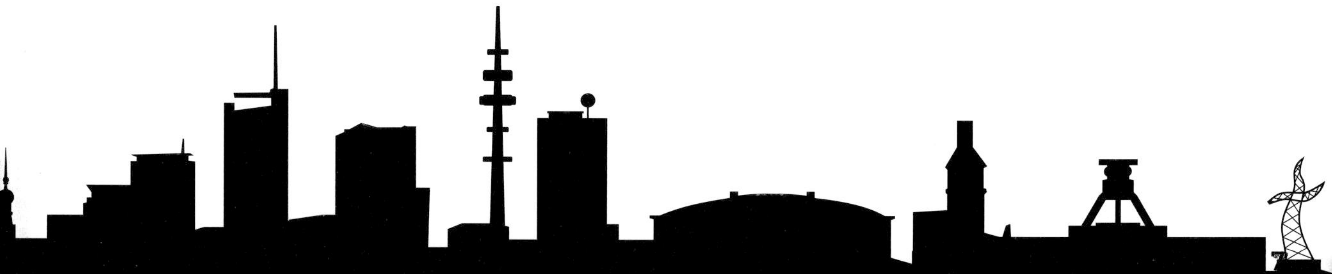

II KLASSIKER 38

III FISCH MUSS SCHWIMMEN ... 66

IIII FRIKADELLEN 78

INHALT

Udo Thies
MARKUS KREBS EMPFIEHLT: DIE LECKERSTEN RUHRPOTT-TAPAS

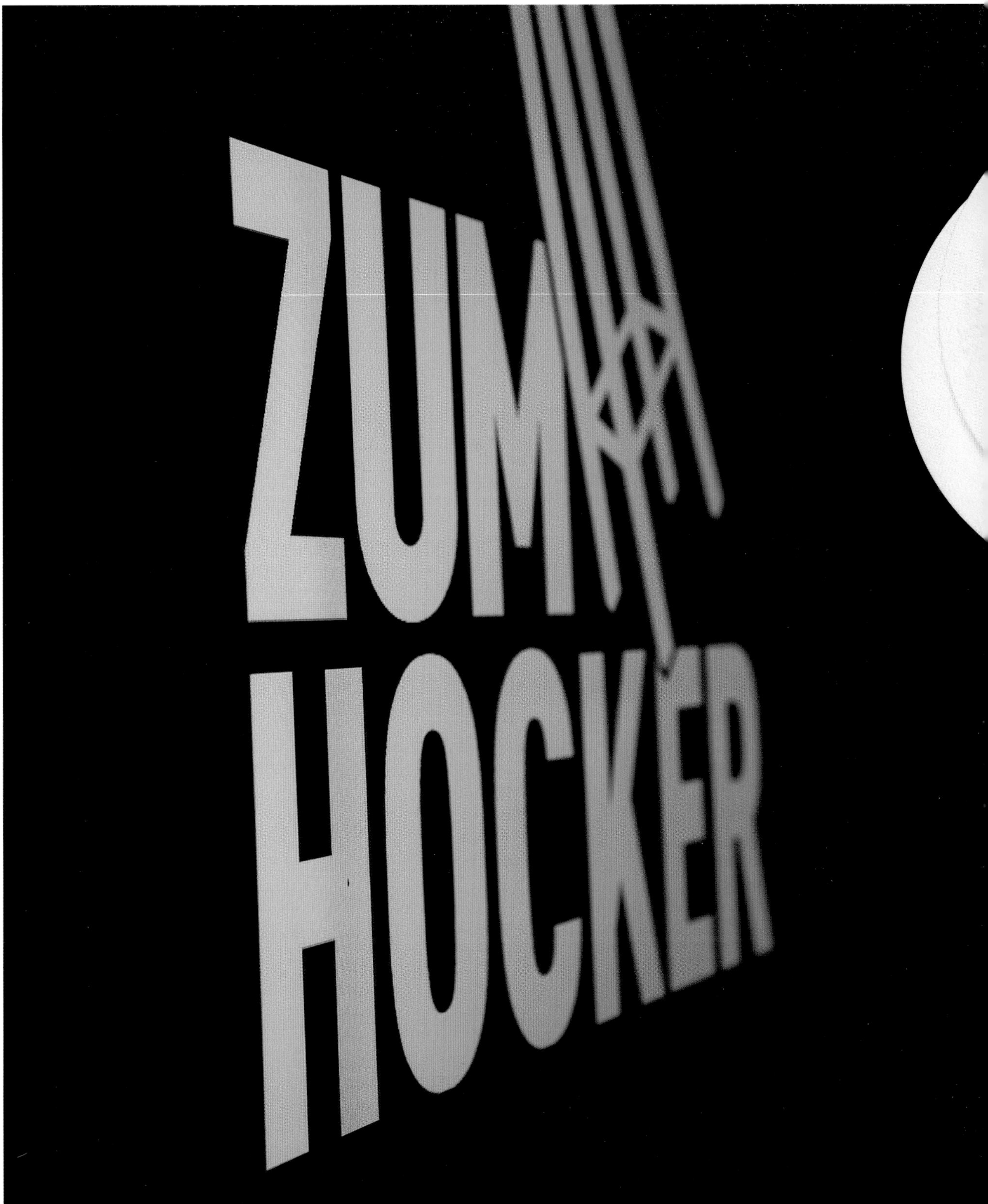
ZUM
HOCKER

ZUM
HOCKER

„MAN MUSS NICHT IN DER BRATPFANNE GELEGEN HABEN, UM EIN SCHNITZEL ZU BRATEN."

- SEHR FREI NACH MAXIM GORKI -

PLAZA

ist ein Imprint der

HEEL Verlag GmbH
Gut Pottscheidt
53639 Königswinter
Tel.: 02223 9230-0
Fax: 02223 9230-13
E-Mail: info@heel-verlag.de
www.heel-verlag.de

Plaza ist ein Imprint der HEEL Verlag GmbH

Autor: Udo Thies
Layout: Lukas Dümer, Dortmund
nach einem Entwurf von Axel Mertens,
HEEL Verlag GmbH
Lektorat und Projektleitung:
Ulrike Reihn-Hamburger

Rezeptfotos: Volker Debus
Fotos von Markus: Nadine Dilly, Frederic Loew
und Julia Feldhagen
Fotos von Udo: Fabian Stürtz
Aufmacherbilder und Skyline: (c) Adobe Stock

Udo Thies wird vertreten durch:
ARTIST & Friend, Tina van den Berg
Spechtsberg 13
D-53797 Lohmar
www.artistandfriend.de

Markus Krebs wird vertreten durch:
S2 Management
Lüderichstraße 2–4
51105 Köln
www.s2-management.de

Printed in Latvia

ISBN 978-3-96664-551-5

Udo Thies

MARKUS KREBS EMPFIEHLT: DIE LECKERSTEN RUHRPOTT-TAPAS

PLAZA